MW01052287

TREASURES *of the*
SPANISH MAIN

TREASURES *of the* SPANISH MAIN

Shipwrecked Galleons in the New World

<small>TEXT AND PHOTOGRAPHY BY</small>
JOHN CHRISTOPHER FINE

THE LYONS PRESS
GUILFORD, CONNECTICUT
An imprint of The Globe Pequot Press

Copyright © 2006 by John Christopher Fine

Photos copyright © 2006 by John Christopher Fine, unless otherwise noted.

The Lyons Press is an imprint of The Globe Pequot Press

10 9 8 7 6 5 4 3 2 1

Printed in China

Designed by Sheryl P. Kober

ISBN-13: 978-1-59228-760-4
ISBN-10: 1-59228-760-3

Library of Congress Cataloging-in-Publication Data is available on file.

CONTENTS

INTRODUCTION

He went the wrong way 'round. With satellite images of the Earth, we now take accurate navigation and geography for granted. In 1492, when Christopher Columbus set sail in three frail ships, few had ventured beyond the Mediterranean Sea and none across the great Ocean Sea—at least that these Europeans were aware of.

The age of exploration and discovery was an age of exploitation and greed. Columbus set sail to find the riches of the Indies. Convinced of his landfall, Columbus called the native people Indians.

The history of conquest and colonization of the New World by the Spanish, French, Dutch, Portuguese, and English is at the same time high adventure and ruthless exploitation. Civilization by the Europeans meant cruel enslavement of the Aztec, Mayan, and Incan people who in many cases had developed advanced civilizations in science, medicine, art, architecture, and philosophy.

Juan Ponce de León traveled with Columbus on the second voyage in 1493. Ponce de León settled in Hispaniola, which is today the Dominican Republic. He then moved to Puerto Rico. It was an age of opportunity when men of daring and a sense of adventure could obtain writs from the King of Spain to set out in conquest.

Equipped with a mandate from the crown, Ponce de León sailed in 1513. Instead of discovering the island he sought in what is now a chain of islands in the Bahamas, he ventured toward the southern coast of Florida, which he sighted on April 2, 1513.

When Ponce de León landed, he claimed the territory for the King of Spain. It was the day of the Passover Feast of Flowers, thus the new land was named *Pascua Florida*.

The Indians were hostile. Ponce de León's men had to fight them off. Some Spaniards were wounded. Native people stole some of their goods.

In this age of discovery the Spaniards found the Gulf Stream. It is a northward flowing current of warm water that begins in the Straits of Florida between Cuba and the East Coast of the United States and pushes water north to about Cape Hatteras; then, meeting the southward flowing Labrador Current of cold water, the Gulf Stream turns east across the Atlantic.

Early explorers recognized the importance of the Gulf Stream and established patterns of navigation along Florida's coast with its flow. It was this route that ships laden with treasure and cargo would follow for the next 300 years.

Ponce de León was killed eight years after his discovery of Florida. He was shot by an

Indian arrow on Florida's west coast. In 1565, the Spanish established their permanent settlement at St. Augustine, the place of sulfur waters believed to be the legendary Fountain of Youth by the Spanish.

In 1519, Hernán Cortés sailed from Cuba and landed on the shores of present-day Mexico. Cortés established a settlement on the coast called Veracruz. Lured by the Aztec's golden ornaments, the Spaniards killed the Aztec king Montezuma and enslaved the people.

Spanish colonization of the Americas brought highly organized bureaucracies. Great wealth was to be made in the colonies, and every ship brought men and women willing to settle New Spain.

This is a story about the lust for gold and treasure, its conquest and loss in ships wrecked in the ocean realm. Of life as it was and as it is for treasure divers who continue to seek their fortunes under the sea in quest of Spanish galleons shipwrecked in the New World. 🚢

THE GOLDEN HIGHWAY

Exploration, exploitation, and colonization followed rapidly upon the voyages of Christopher Columbus, who first set foot on the Island of San Salvador, which he named and claimed for Spain on October 12, 1492. This island in the Bahamas still bears the name Columbus gave it. A spit of land is commemorated, attesting to the place where the Genoese navigator landed for the first time in the New World.

America is not named for Columbus. While the District of Columbia is his namesake and Columbus Day is widely celebrated in the United States and Spain, Vikings long before sailed across the Atlantic and Italian explorer Amerigo Vespucci was given credit for discovering the great lands he found but never colonized.

Columbus made his first voyage in three small ships, none over seventy-five feet in length. When they made landfall, a nerve-weary crew of malcontents, who had nearly mutinied during the discouraging passage across the ocean, were saved by fresh water and provisions to be had on the tropical island. The three ships were in a pitiful state, made less seaworthy by boring teredo worms that attack wood in tropical waters.

Ship construction of the day turned out ungainly and relatively unseaworthy vessels. They appeared for all intents and purposes like a woman's high-heeled shoe, without the heel but with a high poop, stubby prow, and short waist.

Hailed as a conquering hero when he returned to Spain with evidence of the Indies,

Replica of one of the ships of Christopher Columbus at quayside near Barcelona Maritime Museum in Spain.

Columbus set sail again and again, successfully making four ocean crossings.

Discovery followed discovery. Spurred on by the lure of gold and greatness, financed by backers also seeking great fortunes and subsidized by the crown, Spanish explorers became conquistadors: conquerors, merciless exploiters of the New World's wealth. Priests carried aboard every ship likewise conquered horses, and crosses, all of which the natives had never seen before. These ships returned, their holds crammed with bullion and specie, in gold and silver coins, the stuff dreams are made of. Treasure in gold, silver and precious jewels like the *esmeralda*, that stone of green fire, the emerald, symbol of wealth and status at court.

BILLIONS IN GOLD

How many ships? For how long? How much gold and silver, jewels and articles of commerce were carried back to Spain? These questions can be answered because the Spanish kept meticulous records. From 1500 to 1820 there were approximately 17,000 voyages from the New World to Spain. The estimated wealth in gold, silver, and jewels amounted to more than $20 billion. Some estimates figure that 10 percent of these ships were lost at sea, which would amount to some $2 billion left on the ocean floor. These values were established when gold was valued at the equivalent of $20 per ounce.

It has been estimated that between 1493 and 1780, the height of the Spanish colonial period, 103,246,510 fine ounces of gold were produced.

Researching Spanish archives to locate documents, translating them from early Spanish *procesal* script, then interpreting them is an ongoing process by academics who visit the Archivo General de Indias in Seville. Scholars study bound folios, or *legajos*, of handwritten documents that describe the cost and profit, list the ships and the ships lost, their salvage, and itemized bills submitted by salvors.

Archive of the Indies in the old House of Trade (Casa de Contratación) building in Seville.

the hapless Indians' souls, even if it meant stealing their gold and their lives to do it.

The ocean passage from Seville and Cádiz to *Nueva España* and the colonized islands and lands beyond on the *Tierra Firme* became a highway. Ships licensed by Spain and flying the Spanish flag brought trade goods, glass beads,

A wooden cross. Priests brought wooden crosses to the New World and went back with gold and emerald studded ones.

In some cases molten silver would be poured into a sand mold. When it cooled, the resultant "splash" of bullion would be smuggled as contraband aboard galleons heading back to Spain to avoid paying the crown's 20 percent tax on specie and bullion. The penalty for smuggling was ten years as a galley slave. Despite the harsh penalties, many sunken galleons reveal contraband bullion.

The records describe commerce and account for it in specific and painstaking detail. It all was taxed at a rate of 20 percent, the Royal Fifth. It all was warehoused; it all was packed and bundled and transported and sold and hypothecated as collateral for loans made to the king to finance Spain's ongoing wars and extravagances.

A dispatch by the Venetian ambassador, dated September 1567, to the Doge of Venice related the turmoil at court when a treasure fleet was delayed:

There was great anxiety all over Spain over the delay of the arrival of the treasure fleet from the Indies and when the Genoese bankers informed the king that unless the fleet reached port shortly, that they would be unable to negotiate any further loans for him, Philip II fell into such a state of shock that he had to be confined to bed by his physicians. The king then ordered 10,000 ducats, which was about all the treasure left in the Royal coffers, to be sent all over his realm and distributed to various churches and monasteries for the saying of masses for the safe arrival of the treasure fleet . . . the fleet has made port safely and there is great rejoicing not only here in the Royal Court, but all over the land as well.

All of Europe depended on gold and silver that reached Spain from the New World. Monetary systems of Europe were based on precious metals, and since Spain was an agricultural country at the time, imports had to be paid for in gold and silver. Countries that supplied

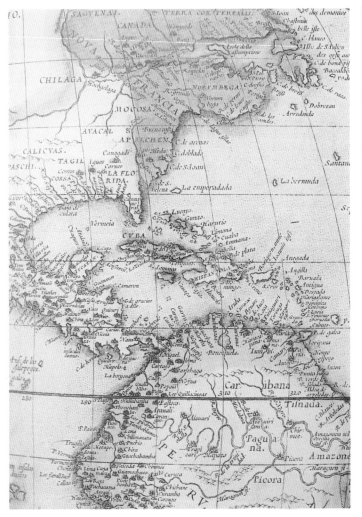

Map showing waters plied by Spanish fleets in the New World.

In case a storm sank a ship, careful accounts were written in three copies. One manifest was kept aboard the ship itself. A second copy was placed aboard the *Capitana*, a heavily armed lead ship in the convoy of carefully guarded treasure galleons en route back to Spain along the ocean's golden highway. A third copy was kept in Cuba, Spain's administrative colony in the New World. The Cuban copy would only be shipped back to Spain on the next year's convoy as a precaution.

The *Carrera de Indias*, the Spanish name for this ocean highway to the Indies, became a seaway of high adventure. Ships were wrecked in hurricanes and storms; vessels were attacked by pirates and enemy nations.

Navigation was, at first, primitive. Rarely did the various navigators in a fleet agree on a convoy's position. As commerce increased and navigation improved, captains maintained precise sailing directions to keep from straying from the well-known pathways over the waves.

Because of the ever-present threat by pirates and enemies of Spain, an Armada of the Ocean Sea was established to escort ships from Spain to the Azores, then pick up returning vessels for the voyage back to Spain. An *averia*, or tax, was levied on manufactured goods and cargoes destined for the New World to fund this protection by Royal Ships of Spain, as the armada was called.

Spain with manufactured goods as well as trade goods for the Indies also attended with interest the arrival of the treasure fleets.

Of course there was a great deal of smuggling. People cheated on their taxes then as now. Indeed, early salvors embarrassed merchant captains when a vessel sank and the Spanish salvage boat brought up more gold and silver than appeared on the ship's manifest.

CONVOYS

War between France and Spain flared in 1537, making the convoy system important for protection not only from pirates and corsairs but also from well-armed French warships. As ship designs changed to accommodate larger cargoes and increased speed, armed galleons were put into service, and Spain established the *flota*, or fleet, system with regular sailings twice a year.

The New Spain Fleet

The *Nueva España Flota*, or New Spain Fleet, would sail from Spain in April, making landfall at Veracruz on Mexico's Caribbean coast. The Spanish lost ships during northern high winds in the Gulf, so they eventually chose an anchorage farther down the coast from Veracruz, behind the Island of San Juan Ulua.

The New Spain Fleet would take on cargoes of gold and silver from the mines of Mexico. Once Spain colonized the Philippines and began trade with Japan and China, the New Spain fleet would await mule trains carrying fine Chinese porcelains, silks, ivory, and spices brought across the Pacific in Spain's Manila galleons to the Mexican Pacific port of Acapulco and then overland in mule caravans to Veracruz.

On the return voyage, the New Spain Fleet from Veracruz would sail along the Gulf for the three-week trip to Havana where the ships would make repairs, take on local cargoes of tobacco, and eventually convoy up with ships of the *Tierra Firme Flota* that sailed from Cartagena to Havana for the trip back to Spain.

The Tierra Firme Fleet

The Tierra Firme Flota sailed from Spain generally in August for Nombre de Dios, a settlement at the narrowest part of the Isthmus of Panama. Swamps in the area were breeding places for mosquitos that plagued the colonists. After 1584, a little southeast of Nombre de Dios, the Spanish established Porto Bello, which was originally named by Columbus in 1502. This port on the Caribbean coast of Panama had a more agreeable climate and was more navigable.

The Tierra Firme Flota would spend the winter in Cartagena. During the early colonial period placer gold was found in streams and riverbeds. The Spanish used native slaves to pan for it. Silver was plentiful and found in almost pure form. These easy supplies of silver and gold were quickly exhausted. The Spaniards began mining operations in collaboration with German mine engineers of the time.

When the mountain of Potosi in the viceroyalty of Peru was discovered in 1545, by an Indian hunter, it was eureka for the Spanish. Potosi Mountain had ore so rich that for every pound of ore, two ounces of pure silver were recovered. Mints were established, and a complex system of metallurgy was put in place to refine the ore. Gold was found among the silver ore as well.

Ships at Cartagena would wait for gold and silver coins and bullion to arrive from Peru before heading to Havana for the return voyage to Spain.

The sailings and convoy system were changed and modified to suit the temper of the times as wars raged, and to accommodate lessons learned about storms, winds, and hurricanes that plagued the fleets.

Ships leaving Spain went south to the Canary Islands where currents pushed them south to the Cape Verde Islands. Landfall could be made there, where stores were replenished and leaking hulls were made watertight for the trip across the ocean. Spanish navigators identified the flow of the equatorial currents and prevailing winds that carried them at about four to seven knots across the open ocean.

Captains used an astrolabe, a round brass device, to measure the sun on the horizon, which gave them an idea of latitude once they left landfall. Compasses were subject to error; nevertheless, navigators used dead reckoning. The trip from Spain to the New World would require a month or two depending on the winds. Navigators would first sight land in what are today islands in the Bahamas or in some cases Martinique or Guadeloupe.

After Hernán Cortés subjugated Mexico and established the fort at Veracruz, Spanish fleets would make Veracruz a port of call, just as they did southern ports along South and Central America as their colonies expanded.

It was on the return trip that many treasure-laden galleons foundered and were lost in storms. The outgoing voyage from Spain along the Carrera de Indias was plagued with anguish in the lack of clean water, adequate food, or medicine, while the return was paved with gold. 🚢

THE 1622 FLEET: THE *Atocha* AND THE *Santa Margarita*

"*They were bringing coins up in bags, chests, and buckets. They had speedboats to go out. The big boats got so much treasure they couldn't get any more aboard. They were afraid they'd sink,*" *Taffi Fisher Abt said.*

Convoy of Spanish galleons heading back to Spain. Original oil painting in the collection of Bob and Margaret Weller. Used with permission.

MEL FISHER'S QUEST

What Mel Fisher's daughter described was the day they hit the mother lode, when her father's legendary quest for the treasure of the *Nuestra Señora de Atocha* was realized. The discovery was made on July 20, 1985, after sixteen years of searching for the fabled galleon that sank during a hurricane, in an area of sandy banks called the Quicksands off Marquesas Keys some twenty-three to thirty-seven miles southwest of Key West.

"They would load five-gallon buckets and hand them up to the dock. A handle would break and the coins would go down into the water. We didn't have time to stop to get them," Taffi smiled.

Mel Fisher's daughter bears a striking resemblance to her father. When she smiles, the same glow of warmth and charm is evident, and her enthusiasm, her father's hallmark, is Mel's legacy, more important than museums full of treasure.

The Fisher dream did not begin with divers hauling up buckets of coins off the ocean floor. But his legacy was sealed by the discovery of the wreckage of two treasure-laden ships that foundered and sank in a 1622 hurricane off Key West. That discovery propelled Mel Fisher, his family, and his team of divers into the annals of world history.

THE DOOMED FLEET

The quest for treasure is hardly a modern phenomenon. It begins with the human desire for conquest and is driven by greed to possess land, its riches, and its peoples. Spaniards sought to own and exploit the New World's energy and wealth—and in so doing destroyed civilizations that had existed in the Americas from the dawn of time.

On March 23, 1622, Spain's Tierra Firme Flota left port and sailed from Cádiz. The ship named *Nuestra Señora de Atocha* was among them.

Spain had sent a guard fleet from Spain as an added measure of security to insure that the 1622 treasure galleons would get home safely. War with the Dutch and rivalry with other nations continued to plague Spain's economy.

The guard fleet ships, under the command of Captain-General Don Lope Diaz de Armen Dariz, the Marquis de Cadereita, left Spain four months after the Tierra Firme Flota. This formidable fleet was made up of eight armed galleons, three escorts, and two *avisos*, or courier ships, and among them, a ship named the *Santa Margarita*.

The 1622 fleet reached the island of Dominica and continued toward the coast of South America. At Cartagena some of the cargo from Spain was off-loaded. On May 24, 1622, the ships of the Tierra Firme Flota arrived in Porto Bello. The trade fair took place, and hundreds of merchants gathered to buy goods for the colonies from the merchant ships. Many Spaniards sought passage back to Spain, and crown officials loaded treasure aboard.

Captain-General Cadereita arrived in Porto Bello with his armed escort ships on July 1, 1622. In the stifling heat of a mangrove swamp that formed Porto Bello's mainland, amidst the stink of human waste and decay from the crowded settlement, goods were unloaded as the armed ships of the marquis entered the harbor and dropped anchor. The trade fair was in full swing. But nothing was ready for the departure back to Spain. There was no treasure. The silver had not arrived.

Getting treasure to Porto Bello to be loaded onto the ships was no easy matter.

Output from the mines of Potosí, in the viceroyalty of Peru, had to be taken by ship north to the Pacific port of Panama. Then it was a fifty-mile trek over mosquito-infested swamp and marshland from Panama City to Porto Bello. As of July 1, the treasure had not even been shipped across the Isthmus of Panama from Panama City to be loaded aboard the galleons.

The Marquis de Cadereita was a military man of action. He knew the perils that late sailings entailed if ships left for the Atlantic crossing after August 20, when the fury of hurricane season was at its height. The marquis immediately called a meeting in the government headquarters with the governor of Porto Bello and ship's officials. Juan de Lara Moran, the admiral of the fleet, and the vice admiral, Don Pedro de Pasquier of the *Nuestra Señora de Atocha*, attended—as did all ships' captains and local officials.

De Cadereita dispatched an order to the president of Panama to send the treasure they had been waiting for, immediately. Reports reached Porto Bello that an enemy Dutch fleet had assembled at a place where salt was mined in Araya.

The presence of an armed enemy that could threaten the Tierra Firme Flota caused the marquis to confiscate for crown service the galleon *Nuestra Señora del Rosario*, a private ship in the harbor of Porto Bello.

The *Rosario* and its owner, a veteran sea captain and the king's commander of infantry, Gaspar de Vargas, would play an important future role not foreseen on that hot first of July

when the marquis and his officers revised plans for the fleet.

The marquis's order had its effect. On July 3, 1622, 200 mules arrived in Porto Bello and a steady stream of treasure began to pour into the makeshift settlement on the coast, to be loaded aboard the fleet. The mule trains carried silver from Potosí, Lima, and Chile.

Accumulated treasures of wealthy merchants and traders arrived. Merchants from the ships sold goods, such as nails, sewing needles, spirits, and cloth from Spain for gold and silver.

Business transacted at the *feria*, or trade fair, was estimated at 4 million pesos in two weeks. The swamp, stifling heat, and unsanitary and unhealthy conditions of the port created outbreaks of disease. Malaria, viruela—the dreaded smallpox virus—cholera, intestinal diseases, and parasites plagued the traders and sailors.

It was reported that 200 bodies had to be disposed of during the second week of the feria because of disease. The marquis wanted to make a hasty getaway from this diseased and disgusting place, fouled by the slop of filthy human habitation.

He turned over 250 tons of mercury to royal officials. Mercury was a royal monopoly and essential to refine precious metals. He then received the king's treasure aboard his ships.

In addition to the cargo of silver belonging to the crown and private parties being shipped back to Spain, forty-eight passengers rode aboard the *Atocha*.

The handwritten script on the manifest recorded by the ship's Maestre de Plata de

Vreder recorded an immense fortune put aboard and locked below in the *Atocha's* silver lockers.

The fleet left Porto Bello on July 22, for Cartagena, then spent eight days loading more treasure aboard. This included 20,000 pesos in gold.

The fleet reached Havana on August 27, 1622. They were already a week past the important deadline for sailing the Florida Straits before hurricane season.

Tobacco, an addiction acquired from the Indies, became a royal concession of Spain. Indeed, tobacco sales in Spain are still a governmental concession. In Havana the *Atocha's* manifest recorded that 500 tobacco bales came aboard, weighing twelve tons.

The Nueva España Flota did not wait for the Marquis de Cadereita with his galleons and armed ships to guard them. They left their treasure in Cuba to be loaded aboard the heavily armed ships of the king.

Holds of the marquis's fleet bulged with trade goods loaded aboard. Copper ingots from the mines of Cuba that would be used to forge cannons were being shipped back to Spain; food and water for the voyage had to be stowed.

Silvermaster Jacove de Vreder's procesal script manifest recorded 901 ingots of silver, 161 gold bars and discs, and 255,000 pesos of silver coins. In those times, when a seaman was paid one or perhaps two pesos a month for his labors, the *Atocha's* treasure in gold and silver amounted to 1 million pesos.

Piloting was as much an art and experiment as it was a science. Astronomy and superstition played a role in predicting weather. Religion often entered into the superstitions that affected decisions about when to sail.

The marquis was an intelligent man—wise to the fact that he had been delayed far too long and his fleet would risk the perils of severe storms once they left Havana.

The marquis and his captains, merchants, and officials consulted the chief pilot of the fleet, Lorenzo Vernal, who described that with the new moon, on September 5th, the Earth, moon, and sun would be in conjunction. Vernal predicted bad weather.

But on Sunday, September 4, 1622, the weather looked so good the Marquis de Cadereita sailed. He boarded the Capitana *Nuestra Señora de Candelaria.* More than a thousand miles away, a hurricane was building in the tropics at the very moment his twenty-eight ships left Havana.

It was late into hurricane season, but the conjunction dawned with clear weather and the king urgently needed the treasure to support Spain's wars and expenses.

THE TREASURE SHIPS

The *Nuestra Señora de Atocha,* a new vessel constructed in Havana the year before, was armed with twenty bronze cannons. It was the Almiranta of the fleet and acted as rearguard. A day out of Havana, the fleet reached the fast flowing current of the Gulf Stream as the weather began to change.

Winds came from the northeast; ten-foot seas began to work on the ships. Even with

The Officers' Ships

There were certain ships in the fleet that had a special purpose. The three most important of these were:

- **Capitana.** The general or overall commander of the fleet sailed in this ship. It led the convoy.

- **Almiranta.** The admiral of the fleet sailed in this ship, and it brought up the rear of the convoy. The Almiranta was a heavily armed ship and could sail from the rear for defense.

- **Gobierno.** The vice admiral's ship.

How Spanish Ships Were Named

Spanish ships were named after patron saints. Sometimes they were named after several patron saints, including the saints of towns and villages where the owners or captains were from. Sometimes the owners were the captains, and sometimes not.

When log entries had to be made, when clerks had to note a ship's name, when contemporary Spanish salvors wrote their reports or submitted expense accounts to the crown, it would not be handy to keep writing the full ship's name in longhand, in the number of copies required by colonial bureaucracy.

Therefore the Santissima Trinidad y Nuestra Señora de la Concepcion *became simply* Urca de Lima. *The ship's captain was Miguel de Lima.*

Or, the name of the ship might be simply shortened. Nuestra Señora de Atocha *became* Atocha.

To complicate matters, a ship might be referred to by the type of vessel it was. For example, the Urca de Lima *was a* refuerzo *(a supply ship). So the captain-general and his other men may have simply referred to the ship in logs as: refuerzo.*

General Classification of Ships Used by the Spanish

- **Refuerzo.** This word means refurbish. It designated a supply ship, often reappointed to be an armed merchant ship.

- **Frigatilla.** A small, fast, armed ship with a small draft that could enter shallow harbors. This general utility ship was also used to carry dispatches.

- **Urca.** This simply meant ship.

- **Nao.** This term was used by the Spanish to designate a merchant ship.

- **Aviso.** The word means advice. The name was used for smaller ships that carried messages from one ship to another, or for an armed ship that would carry dispatches, payrolls, mail, and passengers quickly to other ports, often sailing from Cuba to St. Augustine.

- **Patache.** A small ship, like an aviso.

The author with Mel Fisher. Fisher has his foot on the bronze salvage bell used by Spanish salvor Melián to recover treasure from the sunken 1622 fleet.

reduced sail, the vessels were being tossed around. Smaller ships in the convoy lost their masts and fell behind. One ship, the *Nuestra Señora de la Consolacion*, capsized and sank. The sky darkened long before night.

Aboard the *Santa Margarita*, Captain Bernardino de Lugo had priests hear confessions. Aboard the *Atocha*, chaplains led the litany, grasping the statue of Our Lady of Atocha, which had been brought belowdecks for solace and safety.

The *Nuestra Señora de Atocha* was named for a Madrid shrine honoring the Virgin. Now the precious statue offered the only hope of salvation as wind shifted from the south and the ships were pushed toward the treacherous reefs of Florida.

With the wind's shift to the south, six ships remained in harm's way, within the shoals of Florida: the *Rosario*; a Portuguese slave ship that joined the convoy with goods bought with the profits of selling Negro slaves in the New World; the *patache* of the fleet, or small dispatch boat; the two galleons, the *Atocha* and *Santa Margarita*; and a Cuban coast guard vessel.

The marquis aboard the *Candelaria* with the rest of the fleet got past the Dry Tortugas and made it to safety in the Gulf of Mexico.

As Tuesday dawned on September 6th, the ships in harm's way were greeted by fifteen-foot waves and the distant Tortuga Islands. Anchors were ordered heaved into the sea to stop the juggernaut that would ground the ships.

The *Rosario* grounded and wrecked, as did the slaver and the patache. Forty miles east of these shipwrecked vessels the *Santa Margarita* and *Atocha* tried to set anchors to prevent their grounding in the storm.

It was to no avail. The *Santa Margarita* had lost her mainmast, rudder, and foresail. Captain de Lugo could not maneuver his ship. The *Santa Margarita* struck the reef, and to the east, within sight of the *Santa Margarita*, the *Atocha* wrecked as well.

Without its foremast, the *Atocha* was thrust upon the reef. The force of the grounding broke its mainmast and opened the ship's hull. Passengers and crew were trapped below and drowned. Those who made it up on deck through the forecastle were swept overboard.

The *Atocha* sank in more than fifty feet of water, with only a mizzenmast above the surging waves.

One small ship, the *Santa Cruz*, survived the hurricane. When the weather cleared by morning, the crew began the task of picking up victims of the wrecking. Captain de Lugo survived with twenty crewmen.

The *Santa Cruz* took aboard sixty-eight survivors from the *Santa Margarita*. Only five survived from the *Atocha*; 260 perished. In all 550 died in the tragedy. Six ships had wrecked on the shoals and shallow reefs off the Marquesas Keys scattered over fifty miles of ocean.

The rest of the ships from the fleet returned to Havana. The Marquis de Cadereita wasted no time in convening a *junta* or meeting of captains and government officials.

It was at this meeting that Gaspar de Vargas, now fifty-five years old and a veteran of the Armada of 1588 who had been chief pilot on fifteen crossings from Spain, urged the marquis to take the ships to Spain.

General Juan de Lara Moran agreed with the pilot Lorenzo Vernal that it was too risky and it was of urgent importance to return to the sunken galleons to salvage their treasure.

Gaspar de Vargas was dispatched to find the three sunken galleons. He assembled five ships and left Havana on September 16th.

A ship's captain, Bartolome Lopez, recovered a floating chest from the water containing the horde of a greedy passenger on the *Santa Margarita*.

Lopez discovered the *Atocha*'s mast sticking up from the sea on what he described to the marquis as the last key of Matecumbe. He returned to Cuba and informed the marquis.

Lopez was sent to find Vargas and guide him to the wreckage. They arrived and sent a launch to the mizzenmast, still breaking the surface. The depth of the wreck was taken at fifty-five feet.

It was impossible for Vargas's breath-holding divers to break through the intact hull of the *Atocha* to salvage any of the treasure. They recovered two upper deck cannons and began to look for the *Santa Margarita*.

Vargas could not locate the *Santa Margarita*, but he did sail to Loggerhead Key in the Dry Tortugas and rescued the few survivors of the *Rosario* where it had grounded. Vargas burned the *Rosario*, as was the custom, and took the treasure and cannons just as another fierce hurricane passed through the area on October 5th.

The survivors from the *Rosario* and Vargas's men clung to life while forty miles away in a place known today as the Quicksands, the fury of this second hurricane destroyed the *Atocha*'s hull and timbers, throwing it around in the surge of waves and high seas.

Parts of the wreckage were torn away and scattered by the wind and waves over great distances; some wreckage was scattered over about forty miles.

Vargas returned to Havana with the survivors and *Rosario's* treasure and went again to seek the *Atocha*. The loss of the treasure from the 1622 fleet devastated the merchant community in Spain and the New World.

King Philip IV required copies of manifests to account for the immense loss. The crown would not reap profits from their monopoly on tobacco. Copper to forge cannons would not reach the armories. The silver in bullion and coins would never reach the treasury to pay anxious creditors and support Spain's war against Dutch incursions in the New World.

The Marquis de Cadereita joined Vargas in the Keys to supervise the salvage in February 1623. They camped on one of the islands formed by mangroves. The island was named for him and became the Cayos del Marques, Marquis's Key.

Some silver was brought up by skilled pearl divers from the deep water where the *Atocha* sank. The marquis left the island in March and returned to Havana where he financed the continuing salvage operation before he sailed with the remnants of his fleet to Spain.

Sand drifted over the ocean floor, obscuring the sunken *Atocha* and *Santa Margarita*. Even the skilled Spanish engineer who joined Vargas in the salvage effort, Nicholas de Cardona, gave up hope of recovering the bulk of the treasure. These shifting sand areas occur today and still make navigation perilous.

De Cardona carefully drew a map of the location. Spanish salvors never even recovered the cost of the salvage recorded at 100,000 pesos. They gave up the attempt until June

1626, when Spanish salvor Don Francisco Núñez Melián recovered the first silver bar from the *Santa Margarita*.

Melián made use of Engineer Cardona's map. If he found treasure, he would get one-third and would be able to reimburse his expenses from the crown's share.

Melián fabricated a bronze diving bell that was hammered and riveted. It weighed 680 pounds and would enable the free divers working deep to swim inside it and gasp a breath of air so they could continue to work below.

Melián began a momentous salvage. His support camp was established on a key in the southwest Marquesas, where the wreckage lay offshore of the low-lying islands. He used Indian men who were accustomed to diving for pearls off Margarita Island near Venezuela.

Melián's divers recovered bronze cannons, coins, and silver bars from the remains of the *Santa Margarita*. Melián recovered 64,000 pieces of eight, huge cast bars of silver, worked silver and bronze cannons. Melián was successful where others had failed, and the treasure was put aboard galleons in 1626 and sent to Spain where war and intrigue raged.

Meanwhile, the Dutch continued to invade Spanish territory in the New World and threatened Spanish Pacific trade and shipping. The treasure was needed more than ever to pay Spain's creditors and fuel its wars.

Melián persisted and sailed to the Marquesas Keys again in 1627 and re-established diving and salvage operations in May. By June, they had brought up more silver and cannons from the *Santa Margarita*.

Salvage operations were halted when an armed ship of the Dutch West India Company, towing a launch, drove down on Melián's crew, forcing them to flee and escape to Havana.

Melián returned to the site in October 1628, well into the winter season. He had moderate success, but the Dutch again arrived and engaged him in battle. Melián was saved from defeat by a Spanish ship that arrived from St. Augustine.

The same year, the Dutch decided to mount a major battle fleet to attack the Spanish. Admiral Piet Heyn commanded a large Dutch fleet. When the treasure fleet sailed out of Havana Harbor in 1628, General Juan de Benavides's entire fleet was captured by Piet Heyn's thirty warships and stripped of 3 million pesos of treasure in Matanzas Bay on the northern coast of Cuba.

Melián tried to resume salvage in 1629; however, the Dutch continued to attack his operation and little was accomplished.

Don Francisco Núñez Melián was appointed governor of Venezuela. Melián commissioned Captain Juan de Anuez to continue the work of recovering treasure from the *Santa Margarita*.

It was Melián's petition for reimbursement of 100,000 pesos and his detailed expense reports sent to the crown that led archivist Dr. Eugene Lyon to clues that would eventually put modern-day treasure salvor Mel Fisher onto the wrecks of the *Atocha* and *Santa Margarita*.

Melián's expense reports and the audit reached Spain. They were archived in Simancas and transferred to the Archivo General de Indias in Seville, where *polilla* worms ate into the bound pages until they were discovered by Dr. Lyon in April 1970.

Melián tried again in 1643 to recover the remaining treasure from the *Santa Margarita*. By this time he had risen to the position of governor of Yucatan. Melián died the next year, without finding the treasure of the *Atocha* and with no success on his last attempt to recover treasure from the *Santa Margarita*.

History was beginning to overtake Spain as alliances between France and Sweden shifted power in the Thirty Years' War, which spanned from 1618 to 1648.

Dutch and French naval forces defeated the Spanish Armada in 1639, at the Battle of the Downs. Spain's grip on the New World, achieved by her dominance of the seas, was weakened. The English were becoming a colonial power to be reckoned with in the Caribbean, and Portugal rebelled against Spanish rule.

In 1648, at Westphalia, Spain conceded Holland's total independence from Hapsburg rule. Spain's power was being challenged.

MEL FISHER'S QUEST

Over the past several hundred years, many have sought the fabled treasure of the *Atocha* and the *Santa Margarita*. The galleons contained the bulk of the treasure being shipped back to Spain in 1622, perhaps worth as much as $400 million.

One of those dreamers was born in Hobart, Indiana, a long way from the ocean and the Spanish Main. The eleven-year-old boy was taught carpentry by his father. He built his first hard hat rig to plumb the bottom of a local pond.

Mel Fisher had musical ability. In high school in Glen Park, Indiana, he had formed his own dance band. By the time Mel enrolled at Purdue University's College of Engineering, he was in full swing with a twenty-one piece orchestra.

It was wartime. Mel joined the U.S. Army Corps of Engineers, was sent to the University of Alabama to study, then shipped overseas to Europe.

Mel's fascination with diving continued after the war when he settled for a while in Florida. His engineering skills helped him fabricate camera housings for underwater filmmaking, spear guns, and other dive gear.

Mel may have been uncertain about where he wanted to settle, but one thing was certain; once he got his hands on an early scuba regulator, he was forever hooked on diving.

By 1950, the Fisher clan moved to Torrance, California, where his father and mother began a chicken and egg farm. Mel took courses in animal husbandry at El Camino College and helped with the family business. It wasn't long before he converted a shed on the farm into a dive shop, put in a compressor, and filled tanks and sold scuba gear.

A Montana family bought the chicken farm. Mel was smitten by one of the daughters, a flaming redhead, Dolores Horton, called Deo. Mel and Deo married and honeymooned in the Florida Keys where they dove on shipwrecks.

Deo joined Mel's life and dreams, and they decided to open a dive shop when they returned to California. Mel's Aqua Shop in Redondo Beach was built one brick at a time by the Fishers, from profits they made harvesting lobsters in California waters.

The Fishers lived the California diving adventure. Deo took to diving and soon held the world endurance record when she stayed underwater for more than fifty-five hours. The Fishers had four children, and while the dive business in California expanded with the popularization of the new sport, Mel still craved the adventure of his dreams.

In 1963, Mel met the fabled Kip Wagner. Kip lived in a cabin on the beach in Vero Beach, Florida, and found Spanish coins washed up after every hurricane. Kip began salvage of the 1715 fleet, but in 1963, Kip was ready for the opportunity to expand his operation with the Fishers' help.

A deal was struck, and the treasure hunters would split any finds fifty-fifty. Mel and Deo returned to California, then moved the family to Florida where they began diving and finding treasure on the sunken ships scattered along shallow reefs just off the beaches from Fort Pierce to Sebastian.

Mel developed the mailbox or elbow device, which was fitted over the salvage vessel's propeller. The device deflected the prop wash downward to clear away sand in order to get to bedrock and coral where items from shipwrecks settled.

In that first season in Florida, Mel dove under the mailbox as the prop wash cleared

Diver using a Garrett treasure detector working a wreck site searching for coins.

away the sand. He discovered the ocean bottom was paved with gold. He made the first fabulous find of 1,033 gold coins.

Hard work and persistence paid many dividends. Kip Wagner, Mel Fisher and his family, and teams of divers excavated what was estimated as upwards of $20 million in treasure from the 1715 fleet.

It was a bonanza that began the Fisher legend. Mel left others to subcontract the salvage on the 1715 fleet to pursue his dream. He wanted to search for the fabled treasure galleon sunk in 1622 off the Matecumbe in the Florida Keys.

What would begin as a dream come true for the Fisher family would take them through the most wonderful and most dreadful experiences of their lives. Good fortune would herald their discoveries, and bad fortune would devastate their meager finances; at times, there was not enough money to pay for fuel for the salvage vessels or to pay the divers and crews who worked for them.

Death haunted the shipwrecks, and calamity claimed more victims to add to a roster of the dead who had met their fate in the waters of the ocean.

Intrigue and duplicity by rival salvors and government officials, who vehemently sought to destroy Mel Fisher's finances and his reputation through baseless accusations, consumed Fisher's time and capital.

Divers enjoying a quiet moment, singing and playing guitar aboard one of Mel Fisher's treasure hunting ships. There was teamwork involved in finding treasure. Divers worked for little money to share the Fisher dream.

Through triumph and tragedy Mel, Dolores, and their children prevailed. Their story is one of high seas adventure that no fiction writer could concoct—no matter the audacity of imagination. It is the stuff dreams are made of.

The dream was eventually realized. Searching an area that he thought promising, Mel's son Dirk and his team of divers hit on treasure. Coins, gold bars, swords, silver bars that weighed sixty to eighty pounds with Spanish colonial mint marks and serial numbers stamped into them were found from the *Atocha*.

Dr. Eugene Lyon obtained the cargo manifest from the *Atocha* from the Archive of the Indies in Seville. When three silver bars were found, they bore the serial numbers 569, 794, and 4584.

It was not an easy task for Dr. Lyon to read through a thousand pages of the manifest. Wavelike procesal script spelled out numbers. What Dr. Lyon found in the archive records described cargoes loaded at Porto Bello, Cartagena, and Havana. This was the provenance Mel Fisher and his family had hoped for.

In an entry from the bills of lading, Dr. Lyon read that silver bar *quatro mille quinientos e ochenta e quatro* of 2,380 fines of silver (pure silver was 2,400 on the Spanish scale) weighed 125 marks, 3 ounces. The bar brought up from the site had been consigned to the King of

Spain as the crown's royalty for the sale of slaves in Cartagena. It matched.

The news brought relief and joy to the treasure salvors who had been under attack by critics and challenged by rivals who, through jealousy, had made false accusations about the validity of Fisher's discovery.

Dr. Lyon's meticulous research led him to discover that silver bar number 4584 weighed exactly the amount described on the *Atocha's* manifest. Soon thereafter, Dr. Lyon found information about silver bar 569 that was shipped by a slave trader in Cartagena. That bar was loot from the nefarious trade of a man named Duarte de Leon Marquez. Bar 794 likewise tallied with the manifest.

One of Fisher's rivals, a man who was determined to find the *Atocha* for himself, denied publicly that Fisher could have found the *Atocha*, despite the evidence unearthed by Dr. Lyon. The treasure diver ridiculed Fisher's claim that the treasure aboard the *Atocha* was worth an estimated $400 million and accused the Fishers of salting the wreck site.

Relations with Florida state officials were strained. It seemed that the evil in men's hearts, fueled by jealousy, had no bounds of propriety.

The department head of the state agency responsible for issuing leases to treasure salvors threatened to revoke Fisher's permit when he erroneously accused the Fisher corporate body of not having paid the state corporate franchise tax.

Deo Fisher flew to the state capital with the receipt, and the issue was quelled. Yet, the lack of adequate cash to keep up operations continued to plague the Fisher operations.

There was magic as well. Mel's son Dirk married Angel Curry, a girl who joined the salvage team aboard one of two enormous Mississippi River tugboats Fisher bought. Mel planned to use their gigantic propellers to dig through deep sand over the wreckage.

National Geographic magazine and the National Geographic Society's film department were doing a special about the Fisher discoveries.

Mel's son Kim discovered a crushed gold cup with an ornate dolphin pattern and a lip where jewels bedecked the inside rim, including an emerald that Kim saw still in its setting when he brought it up. The emerald later disappeared in state custody.

The celebrations were short lived. *National Geographic* photographer Bates Littlehales had been working with the Fishers, documenting the finds and activities for a magazine article. He brought his eleven-year-old son with him on many of these photo shoots. One day, Nikko slipped into the water off the tug, *Southwind*, to swim. The surge that funneled water down through the mailboxes sucked him down into the propellers, and he was killed.

The reproduction Spanish galleon that Mel had been using as an office, treasure storage warehouse, and gift shop sank on August 12, 1973. The floating "museum" had many problems, but the leaks had always been manageable. The disaster ruined many of the displays that Fisher put together to create a museum for Key West visitors to explore.

The Fisher business enterprises were being investigated by the U.S. Securities and Exchange Commission, for Mel had been financing his

Diver Tom Ford coming aboard one of Mel Fisher's treasure hunting vessels with gold. Ford is holding a gold bar and gold disk he located with the metal detector in foreground.

operations by selling stock. The investigation would come to nothing, but at the time, Fisher was in limbo and could not sell stock to raise funds for operations.

By the summer season of 1975, the Fishers were operating with sheer grit and a determination to continue.

Dirk Fisher found an intact mariner's astrolabe in working condition. The astrolabe was used by ship's pilots of the time to measure the angle of celestial bodies and, with those measurements, determine latitude.

Experts established that the astrolabe Mel's son found was made by Hope Homem in Lisbon. There were very few astrolabes remaining in the world, and this example from the *Atocha* was in extraordinary condition. It was the single most valuable find made on the wreck site and one of perhaps two dozen astrolabes known to exist.

Bored with his job of recording the coins and artifacts that were being brought aboard, Tom Ford—who was then an employee of a private guard agency Fisher used to secure the finds and would later become one of Mel Fisher's dive boat captains—went underwater. Tom came up with a twenty-four-ounce gold bar.

On July 13, 1975, Mel's son Dirk struck it big again. Diving off the ship he captained, one of the two large river tugs called *Northwind*, Dirk came across a pile of five bronze cannons. The next day Dirk and his crew found four more just thirty feet from the first group.

Proof that this was truly the wreck of the *Atocha* was confirmed when Dr. Lyon matched a number stamped on the cannon to the roster of armament aboard the *Atocha*.

Two of the bronze cannons were raised and brought in triumph into Key West on July 18, 1975, a Friday. It was a day of celebration—and also a day when the direction of Fisher's salvage would take on a different momentum.

David Paul Horan, Mel Fisher's lawyer, had consulted with Dean Joshua Morse of Florida State University Law School. Together the lawyers mapped out a strategy. The state of Florida, after a series of malevolent acts, had agreed with Fisher and his attorney not to take any action when the federal government bandied an old, unused 1906 law called the Abandoned Antiquities Act, which would allow the federal government to claim the treasure.

Secretly, Florida state officials conspired with U.S. officials to apply for a permit to work the *Atocha* site, which would effectively foreclose the Fishers from operating.

Attorney Horan filed an admiralty claim in U.S. District Court for the Southern District of Florida. Under salvage law this "arrested" the shipwreck, the term of art used to describe the legal process, and made Mel Fisher and his company the salvor in possession.

The shipwreck sites of the *Atocha* and *Santa Margarita* were about twenty-three to thirty-seven miles from Key West, in international waters. This was well beyond the jurisdiction of the state of Florida.

For the first time, responding to the immoral and heavy-handed actions by some Florida state officials, Mel Fisher decided to play hardball and bring legal action and fight the state. He won.

Mel Fisher's treasure hunting ship, the *Virgalona*.

TRAGEDY STRIKES

Just as Mel and Deo Fisher won, they lost. Two days after Dirk's triumphant entry into Key West harbor with two of the *Atocha's* bronze cannons aboard, tragedy struck once again.

Anxious to return to the site, Dirk didn't remain in Key West. He offloaded the bronze cannons and returned with his crew and provisions, accompanied by another of Mel's treasure hunting ships, the *Virgalona*, captained by Mo Molinar. Mo was a diver and friend who had been with Mel and Deo Fisher from the very beginning.

Tom Ford had joined the Fisher dive crew and was aboard *Virgalona* with Mo and diver Spencer Wickens. The vessels parted ways once they arrived back in the Quicksands, anchoring at different locations.

It was Angel Fisher's birthday, and the divers celebrated aboard *Northwind*. It was a special celebration since they were all basking in the glow of the discovery of the *Atocha's* bronze cannons.

It was reported later that veteran diver Don Kincaid heard a voice call out to him early in the morning, aboard the *Northwind*. He woke and noticed something was wrong. The tug was listing to starboard. Don roused diver and mechanic Donnie Jonas to investigate the problem.

When Kincaid and Jonas entered the engine room, they found that a toilet valve had leaked and a connector, which shuttled fuel between two large forward fuel tanks on different sides of the tug, was pumping diesel into the starboard tank. The vessel lurched.

Kincaid managed to escape from the engine room, but Donnie Jonas was trapped inside as the tug capsized and began to fill with water.

In a miraculous escape, Donnie, who was able to breathe in a pocket of trapped air in the overturned ship, found a waterproof flashlight floating nearby. He somehow grasped the flashlight in the total darkness and used it to swim underwater, open the engine room door, and escape outside the overturned ship.

Clinging to the hull were Don Kincaid, John Lewis, Bob Reeves, Jim Solanick, Peter von Westering, and eleven-year-old Keith Curry, Angel Curry Fisher's younger brother.

The divers tried in vain to rescue the others trapped inside the overturned tug. But without diving gear, it was impossible to dive down and save Dirk and Angel Fisher and Rick Gage, another diver trapped inside. The *Northwind* sank in the darkness, leaving the survivors clinging to an inflatable life raft.

In the morning, Mo Molinar and his crew expected to see the *Northwind*. When they didn't, they assumed the tug had already sailed out to the wreck site.

Mo pulled anchor and headed the *Virgalona* to the wreck site to begin operations. Mo and the crew of the *Virgalona* spotted the red raft and picked up the survivors.

The tale of survival was full of miracles. Diver Jim Solanick, who had been trapped inside the overturned tug, managed to exit through a porthole and swim to the surface and safety.

Don Kincaid reportedly had been awakened by a voice that called out to him, telling him to "Look out." The voice has never been identified.

Donnie Jonas's hand had found the waterproof flashlight in the darkness of the overturned engine room, and he managed to use it to dive down and escape.

Dirk and Angel Fisher were buried in the same clothes they wore at their wedding ceremony. Their marriage celebration had been held earlier that year on Mel's replica Spanish galleon. Family and friends attended; they all wore flower print shirts for the occasion. Divers and friends wore the same clothes to the funeral ceremony in Vero Beach, Florida, they had worn at the wedding. The pastor who married them officiated.

The Fishers had found treasure; but the tragic cost—in lives, in disappointment and turmoil, in controversy and false accusations— was almost too much to bear. Still, Mel and Deo and the family decided not to give up.

Dirk had found the bronze cannons, proving they had discovered the long-lost remains of the *Nuestra Señora de Atocha*. The Fishers continued their search.

Mel Fisher finally had to move the Key West treasure museum and headquarter offices from the replica galleon, called *Golden Doubloon*. It kept sinking at its dock. With each sinking, Mel and his divers had to move records and files to dry land.

"I lost a lot of my original 16-millimeter movie footage when the galleon sank," Mel said, lamenting the loss of irreplaceable archive footage. Mel had a new office in a conch house on Caroline Street.

Finally, a solid concrete military building became available. It was in an ideal location, at the end of the Key West tourist trolley station. The building provided good security for the finds, as well as room for conservation and preservation laboratories.

Mel was almost constantly on the telephone. "Of course I remember you," he was heard to say as investors called him to check on the progress of his exploits.

Whether or not Mel remembered the many people who came into his life in those days, the tall, affable, soft-spoken man made everybody feel a part of his adventure.

The Fisher family became an integral part of Mel's dreams. Mel's mother worked in the gift shop. His wife Deo not only worked in the office but also attended to many company details that Mel, preoccupied with the search, was too busy to handle.

It was Deo who kept records and saw to it that the corporation taxes were paid and business was handled on a daily basis. Mel and Deo's children were growing up with the legend of their father's dream in their blood.

Taffi Fisher Abt at her computer in the Mel Fisher Museum office in Sebastian, Florida. The foundation operates two museums: one in Key West and another near the 1715 Fleet in Sebastian. Fisher's dream was shared by his whole family.

"When I was seven or eight, when my father was working farther north on the 1715 fleet off Vero and Sebastian, we used to take every vacation in Islamorada or Marathon looking for the *Atocha*," Taffi Fisher Abt said.

"There was a mistake in the translation. First of all the translation was that the *Atocha* and *Santa Margarita* were lost off Matecumbe Key," Taffi said.

Taffi sat before a computer screen in an office behind the headquarters of the Mel Fisher Center in Sebastian on U.S. Highway 1.

"All of the keys were called Matecumbe back then. Over time only two modern day keys, Upper and Lower Matecumbe Key, bear that name," Taffi said.

It wasn't until Dr. Eugene Lyon, working in the Archive of the Indies in Seville, came across Melián's original salvage report that Fisher shifted his search a hundred miles farther south, to the Marquesas Keys beginning some twenty-three miles off Key West and some forty miles from the Dry Tortugas.

"The islands were named Cayos del Marques in honor of the Marquis de Cadereita. Dad was looking up by Marathon. He kept finding these 1733 wrecks, so he kept giving them away and kept going," Taffi said.

Taffi's youthful recollections of one of her first dives into the family adventure follows.

"I was really young. I don't know if they had certification then. I was still a little kid and intimidated by the ocean. I was holding my dad's hand or one of my brother's. It was that initial descent that made me a little nervous," Taffi smiled the same warm, genuine smile that characterized her famous father.

"I remember finding my first coin. It was in 1973, on the *Atocha*. I was probably twelve or thirteen, and I was diving with my dad. He had a detector, and he was swinging it. He pointed to a spot for me to dig. I moved a rock, and there was a coin, a piece of eight," Taffi said.

It all began to make sense. The report written by the Marquis de Cadereita from Havana dated January 10, 1623, found in Spanish archive record Santo Domingo 132, read in part:

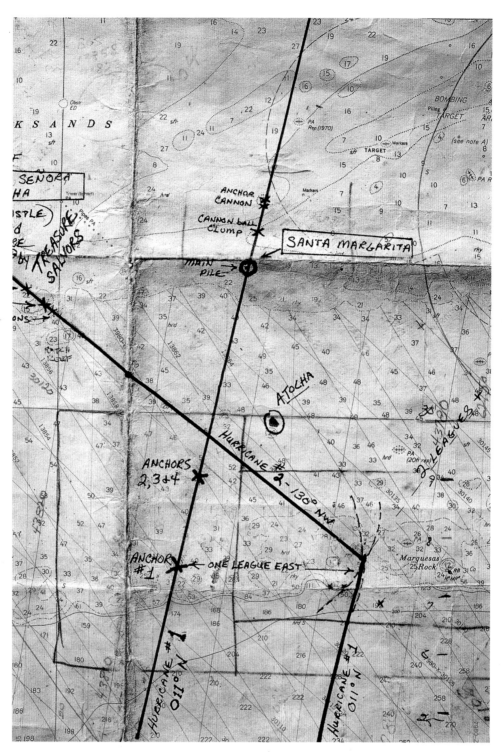

Map made by Bob Weller showing the location of the 1622 treasure galleons *Atocha* and *Santa Margarita*.

*Don Bernadino de Lugo, Captain of sol-
diers and seamen of the galleon* Santa
Margarita, *one of the silver (ships) and
having asked him about it and the other
missing ones, he said that the day of the
storm he followed the capitana on a southwest course until nightfall, when the wind
carried away her foresail. Being at cross-
seas, the galleon broke its mainmast and
the whip-staff of her rudder, and the tiller
was shattered. Not being able to carry sail
and seeing some lanterns nearby, she remained thus until Tuesday, the sixth of
September. Then at dawning, they took
soundings and found forty brazos of water.
Losing the sprit sail which they had lashed
to the foremast in order to go about on the
other tack, the wind carried it away. It
now being full daylight, they loosed another which was lashed on, but the same
thing happened.*

The marquis's report continued its dramatic account:

*Then the force of the wind and the currents
impelled the galleon to a depth of ten brazos
of water where she anchored. Dragging her
cables, she was lost upon a bank of sand,
which is to the west of the last key of Matecumbe, close to the Cabeza de los Martires of
the Florida coast. At seven in the morning*

*he saw, one league to the east of his galleon,
the one named* Nuestra Señora de
Atocha, *Almiranta of the flota, dismasted
of all her masts except the mizzenmast.
While he watched she went down and sank
in such a way that nothing could be seen of
the ship, nor any other thing than half of
her mizzenmast. Then, about ten o'clock in
the morning, the great seas tore his galleon
apart.*

Captain de Lugo was picked up in a shallop
from a Jamaica ship. He marked the wreckage
with a floating mast and pennants, ". . . to serve
as a mark and signal of the place where the two
galleons had been lost. Thus they might be
found, and the treasure and artillery aboard
could be recovered," the marquis declared.

It would not be that easy—not for the hapless Marquis de Cadereita, not for Spanish
salvors, and not for modern-day seekers like
Mel Fisher. The bulk of the treasure aboard the
Atocha eluded them all until 1985.

It took Mel Fisher seventeen years to find
what he termed the "pile," the main cargo of the
Atocha. It was an error in translation of the account of Captain Bernardino de Lugo that mis-
led the searchers. It was written "veste del
ultima cayo." *Veste* was west.

The translator Mel Fisher and Dr. Eugene
Lyon relied on in the archives translated *veste*
as east. The *Atocha* did not lie east of where the
Santa Margarita sank, but west. This revela-
tion, discovered by Dr. Lyon when he reread

Mel Fisher with his celebrated gold chain, his trademark. Each link weighed one ounce of pure gold. Spaniards would wear heavy gold jewelry to evade the Royal Fifth or tax. Mel often draped the chain around visitors' necks and posed for pictures with them.

"Dad had a lot of stockholders. Once a year he'd have a stockholder's meeting. This was the first or second year after we moved to Key West. Dad had the meeting on Ballast Key. He chartered Captain Tony's fish boat to take the stockholders out there. It was Easter break. We camped out two days and painted ballast stones like Easter eggs," Taffi smiled, recalling the incident.

"And of course Dad salted the beach for the stockholders. He put 1715 coins out there and let them keep what they found. He liked to have fun and liked to see other people have fun," Taffi said.

Mel Fisher was willing to try anything. Prompted by a *National Enquirer* editor's proposal, Mel let the tabloid fly Swedish psychic Olaf Johnssen to Key West. On July 18, 1973, they took the psychic out to the site where divers had been working.

As the boat made passes, Johnssen abruptly told them to stop. The Swede then created a séance and went into a trance.

Diver Don Kincaid marked the spot indicated by the psychic. When they used mailboxes to blow sand away, divers recovered a thirty-three-inch gold chain, thirty-six silver reales, and an old musket. Was it coincidence or valid psychic powers of discovery?

Not every new idea worked. One of the more fanciful was the *Squarkometer*. The Squark was designed to give a readout using the most sophisticated combinations of magnetometers and other devices. Fay Feild, a longtime friend and electronics wizard who journeyed in the caravan of vehicles that came

the ancient legajos in the archives, put the salvors on a new tack.

"That one word 'west.' The mistake in translation made them think it was east," Taffi said. The recollection brought a gleam into Taffi's eyes. It was the same kind of pixie twinkle Mel Fisher had when he was about to have some fun.

Divers working below the mailbox or elbow prop wash deflector. The device could blow sand away and dig down to the coral base where treasure settled.

Divers with a gold chain recovered from a sunken galleon.

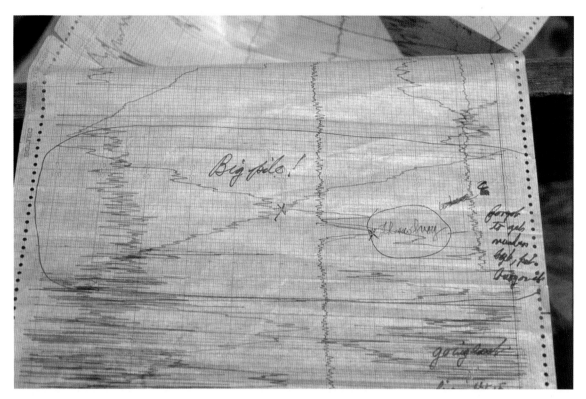

Printout from Fay Feild's famous treasure hunting device, the Squarkometer, named by Mel Fisher.

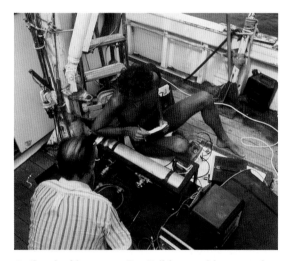

Author looking on as Fay Feild assembles one of his treasure finding devices aboard a search boat.

Mel Fisher and Fay Feild (foreground) studying one of Fay's inventions used to locate shipwrecks.

Ceramic crucibles used for smelting bullion.

from California to Florida to begin the great adventure, helped devise it.

To some extent, the experiments with electronic equipment worked well. In many cases, anomalies and the veritable underwater junkyard, with debris from military weapons testing and bomb practice, made its use difficult.

DOLPHINS THAT FIND TREASURE

Mel told me about his experiments when I was visiting him in the old conch house in Key West. I had been working with dolphins in the northern Keys. One of the dolphins had been bought by a friend of mine and was

kept in a private lagoon in Key Largo. She was an amazingly intelligent animal. The dolphin had instincts that surpassed reason; she anticipated what I would want her to do and did it in front of the camera automatically.

It was truly an amazing interlude to an amazing undertaking. Molly the dolphin showed me how she found coins underwater.

I had been working with Molly for a full day. My heavy motion picture camera filmed the dolphin as she flashed across the lagoon at top speed, passing within a few millimeters of me underwater. The footage was spectacular.

Molly had had enough, though. She grabbed me by the collar of my buoyancy compensator and pulled me up off the bottom and

Molly the dolphin just about to take a coin in her teeth.

dragged me back to the dock. If she could have managed it, and she tried, Molly would have dumped me up onto the little platform.

I took the hint, got my tank and gear off, and just sat on the edge of the dock with my feet dangling in the water. That was fine insofar as the dolphin was concerned.

It was her initiative, her lagoon, and she made the decisions. In a few moments Molly appeared and nuzzled my legs. I stroked her soft sleek body with my hand. The dolphin poked me with her snoot then presented her dorsal fin. The signal was clear. I hesitated only a moment, donned only my dive mask and held onto Molly's dorsal fin.

The dolphin swam me around the lagoon. She would dive down. I'd take a breath, hold on to her dorsal fin, and go with her. Then Molly decided to show me how she found coins.

We surfaced, Molly made a few clicks, turned her head around to look at me, then submerged. I held my breath.

Underwater I could hear the dolphin using her echolocation. Molly emitted a series of clicks directed down toward the sand. In seconds, she located the object she sought. Molly clicked again, snapped her jaws open and closed, which forced a jet of water into the sand to dig a hole. Molly clicked again, snapped her jaws to enlarge the hole and found a coin.

Molly looked back at me, saw I was attentive, turned back to the coin and snapped her jaws, which sent the coin up into the water column. Molly took the coin in her lips and surfaced.

For the next two hours, Molly and I went treasure hunting in the Key Largo lagoon. With the second coin Molly found, she simply uncovered it, looked back at me as I held onto her dorsal fin, then looked back into the hole. She moved her head in an unmistakable signal for me to pick up the coin, which I did.

Mel Fisher was intrigued by my tales of Molly and the dolphins' possibilities. Unlike his divers, Mel would only have to pay them off in fish.

He had known about the ability of dolphins to use natural echolocation to find the fish they hunted for food. When Mel learned about Molly's ability to locate and recover coins under sand, he conferred with the animal's owner, Rusty Nielsen, about the possibility of bringing dolphins to the site to search for treasure.

The theory was sound. Dolphins could readily detect coins and objects buried under the sand using their echolocation. The unforeseen elements in the Quicksands were the currents and threat from marauding sharks.

"We needed pens to keep the dolphins safe at night. The problem was the currents. To keep from being pushed against the side of floating wire pens, the dolphins had to swim all night. It didn't work from that standpoint," Rusty Nielsen said.

Good humored and always ready to have fun, Mel was willing to give anything a try. He and Fay Feild invented and adapted many devices that are now in wide use to locate, excavate, and preserve shipwrecks.

THE TREASURE OF THE *Santa Margarita*

Captain Bernardino de Lugo had fixed the *Santa Margarita's* position as one league west of the *Atocha*.

The *Santa Margarita* went down in shallower water, grounding in fourteen to eighteen feet. While the first hurricane grounded the ship and sank it in the shallows, the second hurricane lashed the remains and scattered the treasure over a vast ocean area.

In 1980, the Fishers found the diving bell of the Spanish salvor Melián. Nearby they found heavy gold bars and thousands of silver coins.

Kane Fisher, another of Mel's sons working on the project, blew sand off the site and on May 12, 1980, discovered six silver ingots. Dr. Lyon was able to match five of the heavy bars to the *Santa Margarita's* manifest. There was no doubt that they had indeed located the treasure of the *Santa Margarita*.

Dr. Lyon matched silver bar 4718 to merchant Gaspar de Rojas. The *Santa Margarita* manifest recorded that silver bar was being sent from Lima to Panama. Dr. Lyon found that the silver bar was consigned to the Brotherhood of the Holy Cross in Seville. Rojas died in the wrecking, but his silver was rescued.

Controversy swirled as a contractor for Mel Fisher put in his own admiralty claim after finding fifty pounds of gold and gold coins on the site.

Mel Fisher with archaeologist Duncan Mathewson studying a printout from Fay Feild's treasure locating instrument.

The U.S. District Court ruled in favor of the Fishers and determined that the subcontractor was an employee and the original admiralty claim of the Fishers prevailed.

The *Santa Margarita's* remains were found about six miles to the west of the Marquesas. These flat islands at one time served as the Spanish salvors' base of operations. Salvage on the *Santa Margarita* continued to yield amazing artifacts.

In July, diver Pat Clyne, who became the principal photographer for the Fishers, discovered heavy gold chains. Diver Richard Kloudt discovered a solid gold serving plate that measured nine inches in diameter and was 3/16-inch thick. Gold was everywhere in bars and chains.

The divers recovered a magnificently carved ivory box cover that probably originated in Ceylon. Historical research proved the possibility, since Portugal, a territory of Spain in 1622, had made inroads in Ceylon at the time.

Mel's longtime friend Mo Molinar, an astute ship's captain who never used a metal detector but whose prowess and special sense underwater always yielded coins and artifacts, dove on the *Santa Margarita*. In one day, Mo found twenty-five two escudo gold coins.

Mo was the diver who found a magnificent gold whistle. Mel adopted the gold boatswain's whistle. From then on, he would wear it around his neck and signal with it when he spoke at stockholder meetings and show the treasure off at lectures and dive film festivals.

A golden belt set with pearls and precious stones was found by diver John Brandon. A portrait painted by Coello of King Philip II's daughter, Princess Isabel, depicts her wearing the same style of ornate gold belt.

Amazing discoveries were being made on the shipwreck sites every day. Diver Rico Ingerson at first threw away a box he pulled out of the side of a hole dug by the salvage vessel's mailboxes. He thought it was a corroded can of sardines that fishermen had heaved over the side. But the box opened underwater and a gleam of emeralds and gold caught the sun's reflection under the water.

Artist Larissa Dillin sketching the intricate design from an ivory box lid discovered by the Fisher team on the *Santa Margarita* shipwreck site. Carved ivory from China came across the Pacific in Spain's Manila galleons.

The box contained a majestic cross studded with fourteen emeralds and a gold ring set with a ten-carat emerald from Colombia's Muzo mine.

The box was silver and bore initials on the lid that looked like LAB, ABL, or BAL. So ornate was the script that it was difficult to decipher. No passenger with those initials appeared on the ship's manifest.

THE MOTHER LODE

While divers harvested riches from the *Santa Margarita*, Mel kept looking for the mother lode, the main pile, the bulk of the *Atocha*'s treasure.

"When we finally hit the mother lode, there was chaos. I didn't know I had so many relatives," Taffi Fisher Abt laughed.

"I was the head of the curating department. My job was to keep track of everything that came in. I cleaned, weighed, and photographed and put the artifacts in a database. We were caught up on work, and we were kind of bored," Taffi said, remembering the events in her life just before they found the main treasure of the *Atocha* on July 20, 1985.

"I had one assistant. I said, Let's get ready. If they find the mother lode, we will only have to fill in the blanks. I thought I was ready so I

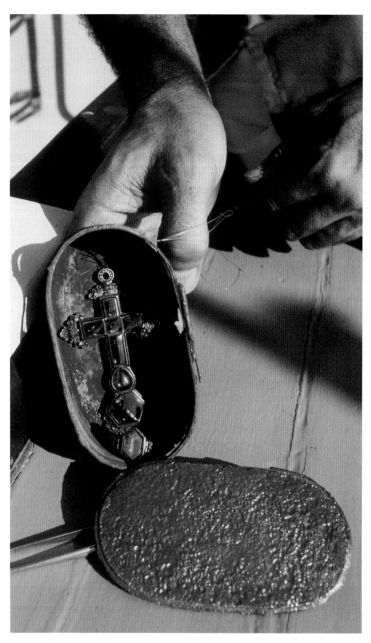

The silver box with the cross and ring. The diver who found it was almost out of air. He thought it was an old corroded sardine can.

The emerald ring. One can imagine supplicants kissing what might have been a high church official's ring. It was found in the silver box with the emerald cross.

Emerald cross found in a silver box with a magnificent emerald ring. The jewelry probably belonged to a ranking member of the Catholic Church who was aboard when the 1622 fleet was struck by the hurricane.

Emeralds. The Muzo mines in Colombia provided the Spanish with fine emeralds. Large crystals with green fire can be worth as much as $10,000 per carat.

decided to research all the coins we ever found on the *Atocha*. I was doing it all with lists, handwritten lists and a typewriter. We had no computer in Key West," Taffi recalled.

"The next day they found the mother lode. It became crazy. Reporters came from all over the world speaking all kinds of different languages. Cameras were everywhere. On top of that everyone in Monroe County came to congratulate Dad. People were standing outside our doors for eight steady months, maybe a year, seven days a week from then on."

Mel realized fame and fortune. He was in the spotlight of media attention and had the responsibility to excavate the *Atocha* site that was yielding gold and silver coins, bars, bullion, and amazing artifacts.

Mel had done it. He had realized his lifelong ambition. To strike it big, to find the *Atocha's* mother lode.

For the tall, good-natured father, for his sons and daughter, for his wife Deo, the lean years, the difficult years, the tragic loss of four lives during the search were justified when Kane Fisher found the pile.

"Today's the day," Mel would proclaim daily, even when things were at their worst, as his ships left Key West with groceries, water, enough fuel to work the wreck site for a few days and hope.

On that summer day in July 1985, Mel could truly proclaim for himself and his family, "Today's the day."

It proved to be a turbulent day and a turbulent year. The find brought treasure beyond anyone's wildest expectations. It also brought trouble.

An hourglass from a shipwreck, used for navigation.

Rivals who were dogging Mel's progress issued false accusations that were reported in the press. Unethical reporters, always looking for an angle, never bothered to check their facts.

Some papers carried baseless stories that Mel had salted the artifacts and that the silver bars and cannons came from other sites—even after it was clear that Dr. Eugene Lyon had matched the serial numbers to the *Atocha's* manifest, proof positive that they had indeed found the mother lode.

Greedy and unethical state and federal officials moved in now to claim the treasure as theirs.

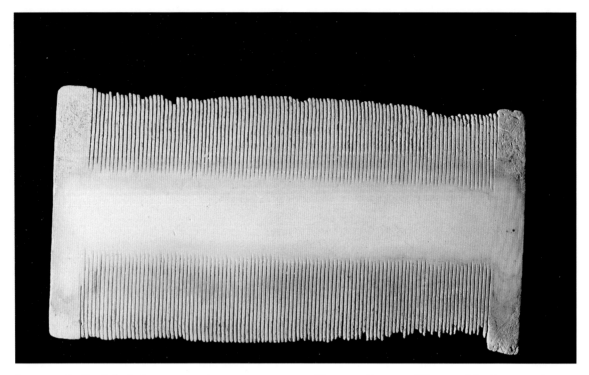

Ivory comb. Lice infested seamen and passengers cramped in unsanitary conditions and in close quarters aboard ship had little water for hygiene. The fine tines of the comb would serve to remove lice from their hair.

Government officials were on television. State bureaucrats captured the limelight, ordered their minions of lawyers and police to claim what it had taken Mel Fisher seventeen years, a lifetime's quest, to find.

During those July days in 1985, however, Mel Fisher and his family were more concerned that his relatively small treasure hunting ships would sink with the weight of silver being brought aboard.

"We got speedboats. The big boats got so much aboard they couldn't take any more. We were afraid they would sink," Taffi said.

"The silver bars weighed eighty pounds apiece. They were coming up in twenties and thirties," Jim Sinclair said. Jim had been working for the Fishers as an archaeologist and conservator.

"Just handling that sheer quantity, much of it heavy stuff . . . The chests of coins were very heavy, they would have 3,000 coins fused together. Eighty-pound bars of silver. One of the chests dropped on the floor, and the coins fell out of the whole fused mass," Jim said.

"The coins on the inside were just like they came out of the mint," Taffi added.

Jim remembered breaking open other masses of fused coins. The outside layers would be worn or oxidized by ocean water; but inside the mass were rare and beautiful coins minted in the New World and looking as they did when first struck, counted, bagged, and placed in chests by the Spanish silver masters when the *Atocha* sailed.

The 2,500-page inventory of the artifacts recovered included: 115 gold bars and disks that totaled 200 pounds in weight; 27 gold chains; 2,615 emeralds, from a half- to 77-carat stones; 115,400 silver coins; 76 gold coins; 64 brooches and pieces of gold jewelry, many set with cut emeralds; 3 astrolabes; 5 navigational dividers; and many other rare and beautiful finds.

Mel, his family, and his team of divers located the remains of the two treasure galleons of the 1622 fleet.

The *Santa Margarita* and *Atocha* yielded up their cargoes of treasure, time capsules that have enriched the knowledge of Spanish colonial history and produced a fortune in gold and silver buried in the ocean depths.

THE *Concepcion*

he Nuestra Señora de la Pura y Limpia Concepcion *left Cádiz, Spain, on April 21, 1641, with the Nueva España Flota bound for Veracruz, Mexico. The vessel had been constructed in 1620 in Havana as a merchant ship, refitted for the Atlantic trade with thirty-six bronze cannons.*

A Spanish galleon coming ashore wrecked and broken apart in a hurricane. Original oil painting in the Bob and Margaret Weller collection. Used by permission.

The ship itself displaced 650 tons and was 140 feet long with a 44-foot width. Captain Eugenio Delgado allowed the vessel to leave Spain already leaking and with a hull that should have been recaulked.

The crown had consigned the *Concepcion* to the captain-general, thus making it the Capitana. Distinguished passengers on the voyage to Veracruz included the new Viceroy of Mexico, Don Diego Lopez Pacheco y Bobadilla, the Marquis of Villena, the Duke of Escalona, and the Archbishop of Mexico. The *Concepcion* reached Veracruz on June 24, 1641.

The new viceroy disembarked in Veracruz after establishing plans, with officials and captains he assembled, for a fleet to be created to protect convoys leaving Mexico against corsairs and pirates.

The new viceroy traveled overland 200 miles to Mexico City to assume his duties while the New Spain Fleet unloaded its cargoes and loaded treasure aboard.

The fleet captain-general Roque Centeno y Ordonez died in Veracruz of what appears to have been yellow fever, a mosquito-borne virus that causes vomiting and hemorrhages. The fleet's new commander was Juan de Campos. De Campos examined the *Concepcion* as its hull was being careened and recaulked in Veracruz for the return voyage.

The vessel was twenty-one years old. It had leaked on the outward-bound journey from Spain. De Campos eyed the lead sheathing that was being nailed over holes in the planking. Wisely, the new fleet commander transferred his flag to another ship in the convoy—the *San Pedro y San Pablo*, which became the Capitana. The *Concepcion* became the Almiranta, the armed ship that would bring up the rear of the convoy.

Brass pistol butt and lock.

The Archbishop of Mexico became a passenger aboard *Concepcion* for the return trip to Spain with his treasure of gold and jewelry.

The *Concepcion* was loaded in Veracruz with specie and bullion belonging to the crown along with general cargoes that included Chinese porcelain.

The trip across the Gulf of Mexico from Veracruz to Havana took thirty-five days, and the fleet arrived on August 27, 1641. Seventeen days were required to load more cargo, make repairs to the leaking *Concepcion*, which had fared poorly on the stormy voyage from Veracruz to Havana, and take passengers and their personal belongings aboard.

Admiral Don Juan de Villavicencio, age thirty-seven, a seasoned veteran of Atlantic crossings, bemoaned the condition of his ship. Villavicencio petitioned Captain-General de Campos for a delay, to effect repairs that were sorely needed since *Concepcion* was still leaking.

It was already late summer and well into hurricane season. De Campos had twenty-one ships in his Nueva España Flota for the return trip to Spain and was anxious to leave Havana. He refused to even wait for the Tierra Firme Flota that was due from South America. It was also a matter of ego. De Campos would have been junior to the officer in command, Admiral Francisco Diaz Pimienta, of the Tierra Firme Fleet, if they left together.

It was jealousy that sealed the fate of the *Concepcion*. De Campos knew the crown was in dire need of the treasure output from New Spain. No treasure fleet had sailed from Spain in 1640, thus the amount of treasure loaded aboard the ships in his command was vital. De Campos knew of Admiral Pimienta's reputation.

In May of 1640, Pimienta had fought and captured the well-defended and fortified pirate and freebooter stronghold of Providence Island in the Bahamas. He had landed with 600 soldiers and routed the English, setting seige to the governor's quarters until the pirates fled. Pimienta captured 600 black slaves and recovered treasure that had been taken from Spanish ships by the corsairs, amounting to some 14 million *reales*.

De Campos was determined to return to Spain as quickly as possible. The *Concepcion* was only out of port one day after their September 13, 1641 departure when a plank broke out and the ship took on water so badly that the crews under Admiral Villavicencio had to keep the bilge pumps working continuously. A signal cannon was fired, and the entire fleet had to turn around and return to Havana.

There were more delays while the *Concepcion*, with her 496 passengers and treasure, had to be offloaded to lighten the ship so the vessel could be repaired below the waterline. Repairs were made, cargo and passengers returned to *Concepcion*, and on September 20, 1641, she sailed with the fleet once more.

As soon as the fleet cleared Havana harbor and headed into the Straits of Florida the weather showed signs of trouble. When the storm struck full force only a few days after the fleet left Havana, the disaster was apparent.

STRUCK BY HURRICANE

When the hurricane struck on September 28, 1641, the *Concepcion* was in the vicinity of 30 degrees north latitude off St. Augustine, Florida.

On September 29, with decks awash with waves, the *Concepcion's* mainmast had to be cut away. All of the deck cargo was lost overboard. Eight bronze cannons were thrown into the ocean to lighten the ship. Nine other ships in the fleet sank, and others became grounded on shoals and reefs.

When the fury of the hurricane had passed, Admiral Villavicencio rigged sail from spars and canvas that were left and maintained steerage with the ship's rudder. They could make some headway but were uncertain of their position; they assumed they were in the northern Bahamas while they were actually off St. Augustine.

De Campos had sighted the *Concepcion* but rendered no aid and eventually sailed directly back for Spain.

The admiral hoped to bring his ship onto a sandy beach where the treasure could be saved. But unfavorable winds prevented his navigation to safety in what is now one of the large Bahama islands. It was October, and by modern reckoning, the ship was west and south of Bermuda.

Villavicencio made the decision to head south to Puerto Rico. The vessel was leaking badly; with pumps jammed, sailors bailed with buckets. In the hurricane, food and fresh water was washed overboard or contaminated with salt water. Unsanitary conditions aboard the ship in the ensuing three weeks caused sickness and death among many passengers who were already weakened from lack of food and water.

A dispute arose between Villavicencio and his pilot, Bartolome Guillen, about where the ship was. Becalmed, they floated aimlessly in now-tropical summer weather, lost at sea without water or supplies. Latitude was determined with rudimentary instruments. A system to measure longitude would not be invented for many years.

The pilot had authority vested in him by Spain's *Casa de Contratación*, the governing body over the fleet system, to determine navigation. Guillen and his assistant pilot Mathias Destevan believed the *Concepcion* was north of Puerto Rico and ordered the vessel to head south.

Villavicencio, his first mate, Francisco Granillo, the ship's owner Don Delgado, and other officers of the ship disputed the pilot's reckoning that the *Concepcion* was east of Puerto Rico, and thus in a safe area to turn south. When the pilot ridiculed the ship's officers, Villavicencio celebrated a ceremony that has become a classic figure of speech in our times.

Concepcion DOOMED

The admiral produced a silver bowl and before all present washed his hands of the decision. The admiral then followed the pilot's instructions and headed the vessel south on October 23, 1641.

The vessel was actually east of what is today the Turks and Caicos, 250 to 300 miles west of where the pilot reckoned.

The Spanish knew of the shoals and shallow reefs north of Hispaniola, which is today the Dominican Republic. A forty-two-mile stretch of reefs and coral heads extend underwater so they cannot be easily be seen.

Spanish charts reckoned these reefs off Hispaniola as the *Abrojos*, which meant *keep a watch*. *Ojos* is the Spanish word for eyes; thus, keep a lookout. In later years, *Abrojos* would be translated as Ambrosia, and the area became known as the Ambrosia Banks.

Seven days after turning south the *Concepcion* struck a reef. The ship's bow wedged onto the coral at 8:30 p.m. on October 31, 1641. The night was lit by torches as sailors examined the damage. Reefs and coral heads surrounded the *Concepcion*. The seas were relatively calm, but the waves continued to work the ship onto the coral.

At first light, a launch was sent out to study the ship's predicament. While there were large coral heads breaking the surface or lying just below the surface all around the *Concepcion*, men in the longboat found that the ship could be gotten off by dropping anchors and cannon and then using hawsers and winches to haul the vessel off the reef, eventually skirting dangerous coral.

The predicament was temporarily saved by the admiral's diligent seamanship. Early in the morning on the second night, the anchor line snapped.

Despite valiant efforts by the crew to throw over a cannon on another cable to catch and hold the ship, they failed to stay the *Concepcion's* movement. With high winds the ship was pushed onto coral heads and jammed forward into the reef with its hull punctured in many places.

When Admiral Villavicencio's account was recorded, he said:

The stern was in five and a half fathoms. The gangway in six and a half, and the bow in seven or eight fathoms. I saw that any further efforts would be useless . . . I sought to place what silver I could up on the decks, but this appeared to all as a danger-ous inconvenience for the risk of the enemy and that it would be more secure left in the bottom of the hold which with its weight along with the ballast would help keep it there, although the galleon was badly holed and broken up.

"The silver was piled up in mounds around the ship," said Burt Webber, Jr. Webber, a diver since he was a young man intrigued by the lure of sunken treasure, undertook a modern search for the *Concepcion* in 1978.

"When we started looking we recalled sur-vivors' tales of gold and silver piled up on top of the coral heads. Gaspar Maldonado was from a wealthy family traveling back to Spain aboard the *Concepcion*. He survived the wreck-ing and gave testimony that the good stuff was piled on top of the reef," Webber said.

When a storm struck the ship with its cowering survivors three nights later, the *Con-cepcion* flooded with water. Passengers and crewmen fought for space on improvised rafts. Many drowned.

Francisco Granillo, it was reported later, threw the admiral overside to save him from the sinking ship. Whatever really happened, whether Villavicencio jumped and abandoned his command or was pushed, Villavicencio was hauled aboard the ship's launch.

Ship's officers in the launch stabbed and killed many attempting to come aboard to pre-vent the launch from capsizing.

Ship's officers cut the launch free of the makeshift rafts that contained other survivors. The launch carried thirty-three people out to sea in deeper water. Villavicencio reached Hispan-iola in the launch a few days later after a seventy-mile trip south.

Rafts were fabricated from wood from the *Concepcion* by other survivors. The foolish ship's pilots sent one raft with eight souls to their certain death heading them west. Two other rafts likewise vanished in the unknown sea. Sharks ate many of the victims of the sink-ing who clung to their rafts.

Some who managed to sail south on makeshift rafts were intercepted and robbed by pirates. These survivors were then put ashore on a barren stretch of Hispaniola, where they survived on wild plants and lemons until they encountered a slave who escorted them to Santo Domingo.

Of the rest of the passengers and crew who remained with the wreck of *Nuestra Señora de la Pura y Limpia Concepcion*, all per-ished. Three crewmen floated away from the wreckage on timber from the ship. Only one survived to wash up on the shores at Puerto Plata on Hispaniola.

About 190 survived the ordeal of the *Con-cepcion's* sinking. The two hapless navigators whose erroneous judgment sent the ship upon the reefs survived on one of the rafts. Contrary to the advice they gave the other rafters, they wisely sailed south and reached Hispaniola. It is said that the pilots sought sanctuary in a monastery to avoid the eventual wrath of judg-ment, and they later escaped.

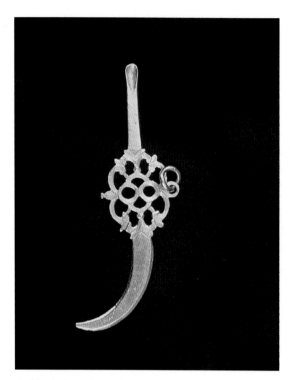

Gold scimitar-shaped pick.

Inquiries followed, and it became clear that the *Concepcion* actually carried much more contraband than had been registered with the crown. Just how much gold and silver was loaded aboard *Concepcion* could never be accurately calculated. Its estimated value was between 4 and 6 million pesos.

De Campos's ship wrecked after reaching Spain when it struck the notorious sandbar at the entrance to Sanlúcar harbor, where the Guadalquivir River ran out to sea and where careful navigation was required to attain the river's entrance for the sixty-mile trip to Seville.

Testimony of the stalwart first mate of the *Concepcion*, Francisco Granillo, who safely reached Seville after surviving the wrecking and who had previously managed to get to Hispaniola in the launch, contradicted Pedro de Medina, *Concepcion's* Maestro de Plata.

The treasure and silvermaster on board testified that a half-million pesos of crown silver plus 550,000 pesos of registered merchant treasure were aboard.

First Mate Granillo testified: "There is much of His Majesty's and much more belonging to private persons that came out of registry because there was not sufficient time to obtain permission and the owners desired more to risk it than register it. The amount which is known to be aboard not counting that of His Majesty is more than four million."

It became apparent that Admiral Villavicencio, who washed his hands of responsibility for the bad decision of the pilots, desired to return to salvage the wreck. The hapless admiral undertook the Atlantic crossing after long delays in obtaining salvage vessels but never actually returned to the site of *Concepcion's* sinking.

Wreckers and salvors plied the shoals in search of the fabulous treasure *Concepcion* held in her holds. Imaginations were inflamed with survivors' tales of silver and gold being piled up on reefs that broke the surface.

WILLIAM PHIPS SALVAGE

Massachusetts shipbuilder William Phips, who did well in the colony's lumber trade and explored the area on trading trips, mounted an expedition to find the *Concepcion*.

He obtained a salvage ship called the *Rose* from Charles II of England in 1683 and searched for the *Concepcion* for two years—but he failed to locate the shipwreck.

When he returned to England to plead for additional backing from the crown, there was a new king on the throne. Charles II had died and was succeeded by his brother James II, who viewed the two years wasted in a futile search warily.

Phips acquitted himself well and fired the imagination of backers at court with his rhetoric about the *Concepcion*. He obtained more investors and set sail on September 12, 1686, aboard the *James and Mary*, a 200-ton ship mounting twenty-two guns, that had been formerly named *Bridgewater*.

Phips also purchased a smaller salvage vessel called *Henry of London*, a fifty-ton vessel that carried ten guns. *Henry* was put in the charge of Captain Francis Rogers. Rogers had shipped with Phips as his mate on the first expedition aboard the *Rose*.

Arriving in Hispaniola in December 1686, winter storms found Phips and his ships trading and passing time in the Spanish port.

When the weather broke in January, Captain Rogers left Phips to his business and sailed with an original survivor from the *Concepcion*, it is said, along with Indian divers from the island. Rogers began a search of the area where the fabled treasure galleon went down.

On January 20th, more than forty-five years after the *Concepcion* wrecked, Indian divers located the shipwreck. It was some eighty miles north of Hispaniola. Captain Rogers returned to port on February 7, 1687, with eight silver bars and two thousand coins.

Phips began a frenzy of activity; ten days later, his vessels arrived at the site. Phips worked the site with four Indian divers for forty days, bringing up treasure.

He was joined by a ship from Bermuda that brought a diving bell. The tub-like contraption was inverted and weighted so it trapped air. Divers could swim inside the inverted tub, catch a breath of air, and swim out again to continue work below.

On May 2, 1687, William Phips sailed for England with the royal sum of 68,511 ounces of silver and a bag of gold. The King of England received ten percent, and Phips's investors were richly rewarded. Phips was knighted by the king, and his efforts made him wealthy.

Phips returned to the *Concepcion* in December 1687 with a partner, Sir John Narbrough. The reefs were swarming with treasure seekers.

The Phips party counted thirty-two vessels probing and digging for treasure on the site. It was a free-for-all melee with piracy and violent confrontations between the salvors. Phips had to chase off the poachers before starting work.

Coral had encrusted and grown over the wreckage. Evidence was everywhere that Jamaica-based salvors had tried to get at it. Some of these salvors landed and declared their treasure on Jamaica.

Phips and Narbrough worked the site, but they found that conditions were difficult because of the encrustations. Narbrough became ill. The day before his death, in a letter dated May 26, 1688, Narbrough wrote to the principal backer of the expedition, Henry Christopher

TREASURES OF THE SPANISH MAIN

Monck, the Duke of Albermarle: "We are finding very little silver on ye wreck and have used all our endeavors to gitt up ye rocks abaft, but find them too strong for us."

The treasure recovered on Phips's second voyage to the site did not reimburse the costs incurred in the salvage. Yet his previous success brought Phips privilege, a knighthood, and governorship of Massachusetts colony.

In February 1695, at the age of forty-four, Sir William Phips, still intrigued by the lure of sunken treasure, was in the West Indies seeking treasure when he contracted a fever and died. Other reports indicate that he died of influenza the year before, in England.

Phips's fame was forever linked to the Silver Banks. The sea floor of what was once called the Abrojos or Ambrosia Banks, was covered with silver.

WEBBER'S SEARCH FOR THE *Concepcion*

It wasn't until November 1978 that Burt Webber, Jr., a diver from Annville, Pennsylvania, located the elusive remains of the *Nuestra Señora de la Pura y Limpia Concepcion*.

Like Admiral Villavicencio and Phips before him, Burt Webber failed in his first attempt to locate the fabulous treasure lost on the shoals north of the Dominican Republic.

Webber teamed up with Jack "Blackjack" Haskins, a retired airline pilot and archive researcher, who had become an expert in reading and translating documents in the Spanish archives in Seville.

Webber, as many others before him, returned—after a $250,000, five-month quest—empty-handed. Webber's interest in the *Concepcion* reached Peter Earle in England. Earle had written a book based upon historical accounts entitled *The Treasure of the Concepcion*.

The English author contacted Jack Haskins and Burt Webber with a new clue. Earle had found the ship's log of the *Henry*, Captain Francis Rogers's fifty-ton ship that salvaged the treasure with Phips. The two Americans, bolstered by the new evidence, traveled to Maidstone, England, and joined Earle in the Kent archives to study the *Henry's* log.

The log of the *Henry of London* had been part of the personal papers of Narbrough that changed hands after his death and were eventually donated—not to the British Museum, but to the small provincial library in Kent. The ship's journal of 1687 read:

At 8 in the morning weighed and with a fine small breeze at South-Southeast, running down Northwest and Northwest-by-North along the south side of the reef. After we passed those boylers from which we weighted, met with very few, and a constant depth from 15 to 16 fathoms, rocky ground and at 11 of the clock, having run down much about the same place where they left off searching, stood in with the reef, 'til our depth was ten fathoms and came to with our grapnel and chain. South from the reef one and a half miles. Had a boyler east of us dis-

tance about three ship lengths. At noon observed and made latitude twenty degrees 37 minutes north. Soon after the boat and canoe went a searching and in two hours time our boat returned on board again bringing us happy and joyful news of the canoe finding the wreck, there being in her Mr. Covell, Francis Ingona and two divers, for which blessings we return praise and thanks to almighty God . . . She lies in the midst of the reef between three large boylers, the tops of which are dry at low water. In some places upon her there is seven fathoms which is the largest depth, 6 and 5, the shallow most part. Most of the timber is consumed away and so overgrown with coral that had it not been for her guns she would scarce ever have been found, it being at least 45 years since she was lost and the richest ship that ever went out of the West Indies . . . She bears from our ship East by South and a half South about three miles off and the westernmost end of the reef in sight bearing West of us and the east most end Southeast by East and a half South . . . At sunset the boat and canoe returned aboard having taken up: 3 sows, 1 champeine, one bar, 51 dollars, 21 half dollars and ten pieces of two, in silver and coin money.

Burt Webber, Jr., is a meticulous searcher—inventive, skilled, and trained in the use of sophisticated underwater cesium magnetometers, side-scan sonar, and the use of photo mosaics derived from aerial mapping to locate anom-alies underwater. Like Phips before him, Webber set out in search of the *Concepcion* only after painstaking work that brought him very close to being the one who discovered both the *Atocha* and *Maravillas*.

After both the *Atocha* and *Maravillas* eluded Webber, Jack Haskins had said, "What about Phips's galleon?" It was not referred to as the *Concepcion*. It was doubtful that Phips even knew it was the *Concepcion*. Jack Haskins's attitude was this: "We know as salvagers the technology they were capable of then, and we know our salvage technology now. If the *Concepcion* site can be found, there's a lot of treasure left."

Webber is one of those articulate speakers who can enthrall listeners when he mixes history and his passion for discovery and underwater exploration with emotion. He had spent years and a lot of money seeking two legendary treasure galleons that eluded him, only to be found by others: the *Atocha*, by the legendary Mel Fisher, and the *Maravillas*, by the Bob Marx group.

Was Webber prepared to seek yet another legendary galleon that had been the quest of many of the most notable treasure hunters since the days of William Phips?

"In 1687–1688, Phips recovered a lot of treasure. I said, 'Would there be anything out there?'" Webber said, remembering his thoughts when the idea was first discussed.

"It was a challenge. The site was eighty-five miles to the closest port in the Dominican Republic. It was located in what the English called the north riff, represented on the best navigational charts today as three inches with no resolution to correlate anything by description," Webber recalled.

"The Spanish didn't even know where they were. The best Spanish description meant nothing without research of the reefs," Webber said.

Undaunted by challenges presented by the project, Webber raised funds from investors—akin to the Phips's undertaking with his investors—and began his first expedition.

"At a cost of 18,000 dollars we produced an aerial mosaic mapping the north reef in color. Now we could see. Now we could correlate historical data with the reefs," Webber said, producing a map and indicating the area of their search.

"Here's the Silver Shoals today. A bunch of little X marks. Very inaccurate," he said, studying the photo mosaic as if the rediscovery brought him new insight.

"The reef is sixteen miles. Half Moon Reef is right here. We didn't have the log of the *Henry* on our first expedition," Webber said. "We only had Phips's log."

"When Phips arrived in Puerta Plata, he traded with the Spanish while Captain Rogers went out with the *Henry of London* to reconnoiter. On the first reconnoiter, the *Henry* found the wreck site. Captain Rogers came back to Puerta Plata and told Phips." Webber's eyes held enthusiasm, reliving that first discovery.

"The reefs look like brown lily pads floating on the water. Some are the size of an average living room, some the size of a football field. What we did was use Mylar overlays," Webber explained.

Two members of his team, Henry Taylor and Duke Long, began the tedious process of tracking the coral heads, numbering them with floating markers and recording the data. "We could come back to them with a smaller reef boat, survey around the coral head and across the channel to the next coral head," Webber said.

Webber and his team of divers found thirteen wrecked ships of various dates but did not find the *Concepcion*.

"The *Concepcion* was a weak target. The anchors were off the ship, thrown over. I know the day we went right over it and never saw it. Had someone been in the water that particular day they would have seen the ballast stones down there," Webber said.

Webber contracted with the government of the Dominican Republic in 1977 to search and recover treasure and artifacts. The split would be fifty-fifty; however, the Dominican Republic would have the patrimonial right to all artifacts found. Everything of archaeological or historical significance would be left in the Dominican Republic. Coins would be shared.

"We spent five months doing circumference surveys. We'd be out on the site two weeks, back in port three days. We chartered the sixty-five-foot ship *Big G* out of Islamorada, Florida. At the end of five months we didn't find it. Just push, push, push. We all ended up with ciguatera poisoning from eating fish we speared to supplement the diet while on site. We didn't know what we had," Webber explained.

"Eating fish out there three days out of seven. Eating grouper, not big grouper. The fish ate other coral-eating fish; we were all about done in. I came back demoralized, sick with that fish poisoning," Webber said.

Delicate Chinese porcelain cup with a hand-painted junk recovered from a Spanish Pacific Manila galleon that sank in 1724.

Burt Webber (foreground) and Bob Weller beneath the oil painting of a shipwreck coming ashore examining a Spanish sword constructed from three pieces obtained from three different Spanish shipwrecks.

Burt Webber studying documents about the *Concepcion*, the fabled treasure wreck he found off the Dominican Republic.

"Jack Haskins sat in an armchair and tried to figure out what we missed. Jack knew Victoria Staples Johnson from pulling legajos in the Spanish archives in Seville. Jack talked to her since she was looking for the same legajos on the *Concepcion*," Webber's face was animated as he described what was to become the break they were looking for.

"Victoria told Jack that she was commissioned by an English historian Peter Earle, who attained an English knighthood and was doing a book on Phips. Jack said he'd like to get in contact with Peter Earle in London. I said to Jack, 'We're done. We're never going back to the Silver Shoals. We have a lot of data, give it to him.' Peter Earle was very grateful. He said,

'By the way, I found the log of the *Henry*.'" Burt Webber's face lit up as if he was hearing the news for the first time, telling the tale again.

"The *Henry of London* was the ship that made the first recovery of the *Concepcion's* treasure. Peter Earle found the log in the Maidstone library. The log documented the voyage of the *Henry* from 1686 when they left to 1687. The reason the ship's journal was not found before was because it was in Lord Romney's estate library. They were investors in the original Phips expedition. So he ended up with the journal as a keepsake. Lord Romney's estate was sold off and the books and manuscripts donated to Maidstone Library where they lived," Webber said.

The journal of the *Henry*, recited earlier, described how they went down the reef. It gave bearings from their anchorage to the east and from there to where they found the *Concepcion*.

"I had aerial mosaics so I knew where they could and could not anchor," Webber gestured with his hands. He spread the maps and mosaics out before him. In the next instant Webber pulled out his wallet and removed a little laminated card that showed aerial photos of coral heads. They looked like so many mushroom caps. The English salvors called them *boylers* since water surged around the coral heads, boiling up.

"Here it is. I keep this in my wallet as a memento. The *Concepcion* was found right here," he said.

"Here is the triangulation. This is the only place," he added, illustrating it on the photo mosaic.

Webber took his research to Annapolis. Navy authorities told him that for 1687, magnetic deviation would be off 2 percent.

"I came up with the wreck here," Webber pointed to the map. "I was off by fifty yards."

Webber had collaborated with a company that manufactured cesium magnetometers. He adapted and improved them and became a consultant for their underwater technology program.

Magnetometers towed by boats on the surface would not work among the coral heads of Silver Shoals. It was difficult to navigate around the giant coral heads and control the depth of the tow fish, the underwater sensor that was pulled behind the boat to detect magnetic anomalies underwater.

There were sandy valleys between the coral heads, and there were irregular underwater islands of coral that loomed up toward the surface, many awash at low tide.

Burt Webber created diver-controlled cesium magnetometers. The devices were housed in waterproof cases; the probe, likewise waterproof, stuck out on its long arm. As a diver swam underwater, the magnetometer could be positioned to any depth.

"I was going around doing circumference searches around Turtle Reef. As I came around, the magnetometer started to pick up a signal. I had an LED readout and headset on. I was about to swing to the northwest. As I made the turn, I ran out of it. I went back and made the turn again. It branched off to the north," Webber related.

"There was nothing much to see underwater. Then I saw ballast. Typical creek bed rocks.

Silver coins. Legendary pieces of eight and screw press coins. The stuff dreams are made of.

One here, one there. What happened was when I got into the area the magnetometer was very active. It took me under a bridge between two walls of coral. I thought it was broken. I surfaced and was picked up by one of our seventeen-foot reef boats," Webber smiled.

He was about to make the most amazing discovery in the annals of maritime history. At the moment, he doubted the veracity of his magnetometer readings that pointed to his lifelong dream.

Webber checked his magnetometer and returned to the site of the high readings. "I went back in there. It was late afternoon. I used ferrous and non-ferrous metal detectors."

Concepcion TREASURE FOUND

Webber had a support diver with him to mark sites that gave readings. He described what happened. "Jim Nace, a neighbor from Pennsylvania, was swimming over the coral head. He pried a ballast rock out. He wanted it as a souvenir. An eight reale coin fell off the rock. Jim swam over and handed it to me. That was the first coin we found from the Concepcion.

"The detectors didn't stop. I got into what we called the treasure cave. It was walls of silver. As the *Concepcion* sank and the stern came cascading down, chests of coins came tumbling out. In eleven months we took 50,000 coins out of that treasure cave," Webber's expression was animated as he related his discovery.

"There were eight, four, and two reale silver coins. Small finger bars of silver, silver bars. No gold; it was all silver."

Webber now pondered the journal of the *Henry*. "Sitting on boats it didn't fit the description that Captain Rogers made as three coral heads. It didn't matter, we were finding treasure. Here was a main site in forty-five feet of water."

While Webber and other divers on his team were busy pulling up silver coins from the treasure cave, Jack Haskins and Duke Long decided to snorkel.

The experienced divers decided to reconnoiter out from the site. "They saw an area a little deeper where coral heads were awash at low tide. Jack and Duke were the first to see ballast on top of a coral head."

What did it mean? Could this be the site that survivors described as being the place where treasure was piled on top of the coral by the crew after *Concepcion* struck the reef?

"When Phips came back to the site in 1688, everybody was working the wreck. They were killing each other, shooting at rival divers. Phips's second expedition was a financial failure. They didn't recover enough treasure to even pay expenses," Webber said.

"Most of the treasure in some parts of the ship was removed when they made rafts. They tore the ship apart to make rafts. It was reported that they piled the treasure so high out there on the coral heads they could walk around on it. Phips didn't say it, but Narbrough said, 'We looked for treasure the Spanish layed along the top of the reefs.' Water was up to their knees at high tide, and at low tide the coral heads were awash.

"The privateer that captured and stripped the *Concepcion's* survivors found out where the

Silver pieces of eight. The legendary coins were even used as legal tender in the United States until banned by Congess in 1857. An ordinary seaman would earn one piece of eight for a month's labor in early Spanish colonial times.

Concepcion wrecked. The corsair had been watering on Savannah. When Phips got there forty-five years later, there was no treasure on top of the reef. Nothing on the reef," Webber said.

"The English corsair got there, took the treasure off the reef. They knew that there was treasure below but couldn't carry it. Nobody ever came back to the site. Why? We think the corsair sank. There is a reef fourteen miles to the south where coral heads are two feet under the surface at low tide. At high tide the reefs are four to five feet under the surface. They will take a hull right out of a ship," Webber said.

"I believe the corsair is down on the south reef. They would have come back for the treasure. It was the real mother lode," Webber speculated.

"The last English expedition in 1690 was a real loss. They believed the stern of the *Concepcion* was lodged inside a coral head. They didn't know that the stern separated. That was the real mystery. In 1690, using cannon balls filled with powder, they tried to fracture the coral head. We found the exploded cannon balls on the site. They failed to blow it open. That was the last anyone had seen that coral head until November 1978," Webber said.

"Survivors' accounts that there was treasure piled on top of the reef were true. There are holes in the coral heads. We couldn't get magnetometer reading on the top or sides. After working the treasure cave we fragmented a coral head with explosives. We set the charges in the evening and detonated them, then went back to the ship.

"The next morning I rolled back over the side of the inflatable reef boat. There underwater on a shelf were layers of coins. An astrolabe was just laying there, fused to it were pieces of eight," Webber said.

A navigator's astrolabe is priceless. Very few are in museum collections. Burt Webber's team later found two more of the rare navigational astrolabes in good condition.

"On one the sighting vein and ring on the top that the navigator would hold it by were missing. We found the ring later in the same area," Webber said.

"When diver Jim Nace came up with the astrolabe, he said, 'Look. There was somebody here before us. Here's a pulley wheel off an air compressor,'" Webber shook his head and smiled as he recalled the incident.

The astrolabe was dated 1618 and made by a famous maker of the time called Diaz. All of the astrolabes and other ships' accoutrements were given to the Dominican Republic and were conserved and put on display in their national museum.

"As we moved into the reef we found an ivory figurine of the Christ child holding the world. We found candlesticks, silver plates. Duke Long came back to our support ship and said to me, 'Grab my lunch kettle, Burt.'"

"It was heavy. I opened it. Inside was a complete astrolabe and pieces of eight in clumps," Webber said.

Webber and his team found very little gold on the shipwreck site. "We found two gold chains. Exquisite chains. Both in the same hole. There was also part of a spiral earring and rosary pieces. Gaspar Maldonado, from a wealthy family who was traveling back to Spain on the *Concepcion*, testified that the good stuff was piled on top of the reef. While Phips recovered thirty-six tons of silver, he only got twenty-six pounds of gold. Where did the gold go?"

Burt Webber is convinced that the corsairs that stripped the survivors on the raft of their belongings, and found out about the treasure, located the wreckage and took it, then wrecked themselves.

The survivors would have also taken gold with them. "Gold was sixteen to one in value for the same weight in those days to silver. They would have taken gold," Webber said.

TREASURE AND ARTIFACTS PRESERVED

The bounty from the *Concepcion* was presented to the government of the Dominican Republic by Webber and his team.

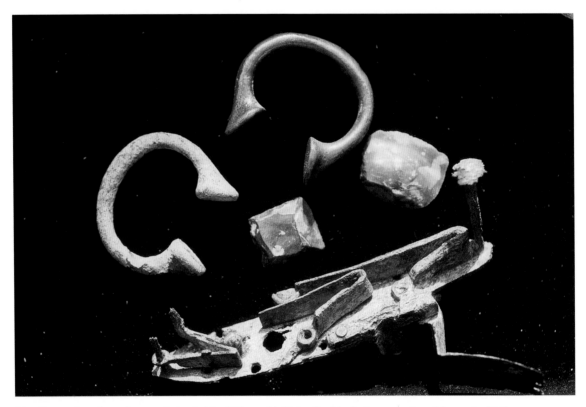

Manilas or slave bracelets, each traded to African chieftains for black slaves captured from rival tribes; a flintlock action from a firearm; and pieces of flint all recovered from Spanish galleons. The Spanish were slavers, first using Indian labor then importing black slaves from Africa to work in their mines in the New World.

"Technically all things recovered from a shipwreck are artifacts. We found many culturally oriented things like Ming dynasty ware, serving plates, three astrolabes. All of those things were part of their 50 percent, and they were declared part of the Dominican Republic's National Patrimony. Once they were conserved and cleaned, they were put in the national museum," Webber said.

"We had a division with the government. We ended up with our 50 percent in coins and bullion. We got half of the 60,000 coins and silver bullion. Our coins had a higher numismatic value as an offset of the value of the artifacts they retained."

"We signed off on a value for the gold chain at $250,000. The appraisals were very conservative as we know now. When the Dominican Republic let us take the gold chain out of the country, appraisal experts said that as a one-of-a-kind pedigreed find from that galleon we could have had a closed auction of only the top clients of Neiman Marcus and the chain, they said, would have gone for a million dollars," Webber concluded.

"They were not for sale. In the long run, that was beneficial. There is always the debate between private sector exploration of shipwrecks versus academia. If all this stuff disappears into private hands, it is not beneficial to

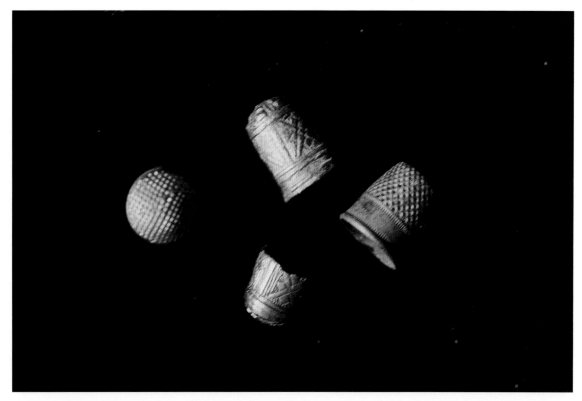

Thimbles that were brought from Spain. Simple goods had to be imported to the New World, and traders and merchants licensed by the crown would conduct business selling manufactured goods shipped from Spain. They bought or traded for goods from the Indies.

the public interest. There is no opportunity to study it and view it. In the case of the *Concepcion*, what I recovered became part of the National Patrimony of the country and was retained by the national museum," Webber said.

Burt Webber, Jr., and his team of divers and researchers located and excavated one of the most important shipwrecks in the history of the Spanish Main. The quest, driven by the persistence and acumen of one man, whose travail led to the discovery only after years of failure, is a triumph for all who would dare to dream about one day finding treasure beneath the sea.

Silver Buddha, evidence of the trade with China and the Orient. The Buddha came across the Pacific Ocean on a Manila galleon, was off-loaded in Acapulco on Mexico's Pacific coast then transported across Mexico to Veracruz where it was loaded aboard a galleon heading back to Spain. It was recovered from a galleon of the 1733 fleet.

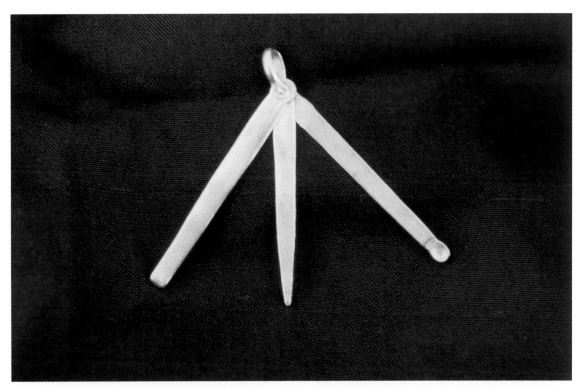

Spanish nobles used all manner of grooming tools fashioned from gold. Ornate tooth and ear picks came up with the sunken treasure.

THE *Maravillas*

The Nuestra Señora de las Maravillas *had been part of a Tierra Firme Fleet of ten ships that sailed from Spain to the New World on May 16, 1654. The Capitana of the fleet was commanded by the Marques de Montealegre. The* Nuestra Señora de las Maravillas *was commanded by Admiral Mathias de Orellana and was the Almiranta of the fleet. Both of these armed galleons mounted fifty-eight cannons made of bronze.*

Rendition of Spanish ships engaging each other in battle.

The vessels of the fleet arrived in New Granada, Cartagena, Colombia, on August 22, 1654, after a ninety-five-day voyage. The vessels were loaded with silver from the Potosi mint and other treasure. They then sailed to Panama and arrived at Porto Bello on March 25, 1655. The ships were loaded with more treasure before they sailed to Havana on July 3, 1655.

The voyage was uneventful until the fleet saw sails off Punta de Pedras, Cuba, fourteen days out of Panama. They assumed the ships were English so turned around and sailed to the Spanish anchorage behind an island south of Veracruz, arriving on August 2, 1655. The fleet sailed again for Havana on September 7th, and arrived in Havana on October 10, 1655, where the ships were prepared for the ocean voyage back to Spain.

Cuban shipwrights refitted the *Maravillas*'s deck knees and braces, replaced the ship's rudder, and cleaned its hull of algae and marine growth. It wasn't until Saturday, January 1, 1656 that the *Maravillas*, along with the rest of the ships in the returning Tierra Firme Fleet, left Havana.

Father Diego Portichuelo de Rivadeneyra was one of the passengers on board the *Maravillas*. He was a priest of the Holy Metropolitan Church in Lima, Peru. He was not an unusual passenger. By the time the *Nuestra Señora de las Maravillas* sailed in a fleet of ships from Havana to return to Spain in 1656, the Spanish had established more than 70,000 churches and 500 monasteries and convents in the New World among their 200 cities. Lima

The late Harry Cox, of Bermuda, with a Spanish octant.

and Mexico City, with burgeoning populations of 100,000 Spaniards each, were larger than even the largest cities in Spain at the time.

Father Rivadeneyra was one of only forty-five passengers and crew out of 650 to survive the wrecking of the *Maravillas*. The priest gave an account of the tragedy that befell his ship in careful Spanish prose:

The Marquis of Monte Alegre sailed with his galleons from the port of Havana on Saturday, January 1, 1656. Following him

were the ships of his fleet: the Gobierno *under the command of Don Diego de Ibarra, the galleon* Jesus Maria *belonging to Don Juan de Hoyos, the tender of the* Margarita, *the tender of* Don Mendo de Contreras, *the tender of the galleon* Pedro Rodriguez, *two frigates that were going to Caracas and Cartagena, and the Almiranta (the* Maravillas*) under the command of Don Mathias de Orellana and which I boarded in Puertobello. We set sails in such favorable weather that we all foresaw a very happy voyage. The Almiranta was at full sail and at low prow in order to be faster, all made possible by her new sails, and even though her sails had less canvas than the other ships, she sailed so fast that she passed the Capitana.*

The priest was sick for four days and stayed in his cabin until Tuesday when the voyage continued in good weather and the ships made for the Bahamas Channel. Father Rivadeneyra continued his account:

We were also anticipating the enjoyment of the games and festivities that were to take place the next night (the day of Epiphany). The felicities of life, said a Gentile philosopher, are shadows on which man's great ruins are reflected. And shadows were the enjoyments and mental rejoicings, and palpable reality and experienced pain were the final judgment that within four hours would befall the Almiranta, the 650 men aboard her, the five million pesos in gold and silver, the granary, sugar, hides, skins, and brazil-wood that she carried in her holds.

The priest fell asleep after dinner and was awakened by shouts on deck; from the bow, the boatswain saw shallow water. The priest's account continued:

As I learned later, they found that the waters were whitish and awashing, which are indications that the bottom is near, and that their sounding revealed 13 fathoms. Everyone was in an uproar, and I jumped from the bed, dressed hurriedly and went on deck where I found some alarmed, others confused, and everyone giving opinions about what should be done. And in the midst of much discussions and contradictions a cannon shot was fired to alert the fleet about where we were and of the danger we were facing. All its ships were rather far behind us. As I subsequently learned, this was because their pilots thought that the passage through the strait of the channel had already taken too long. As such, as soon as they heard the cannon shot they changed course for Florida in order to have better

passage and depths than those of the Capitana and Almiranta, which were sailing at a small distance from each other.

The priest now recounted the fateful misunderstanding that sealed the fate of the *Nuestra Señora de las Maravillas* forever.

However, the galleon of Don Juan de Hoyos continued on her course toward the shoals because her pilot thought that the cannon fired by the Capitana was meant to signal that she was shifting more windwardly to improve her sailing, as she had been sailing rather leewardly before. On that course, the galleon's rudder bumped against a rock with such force that it was turned loose from its gudgeon and truss and fell into the sea. As a result, the galleon went aground in 4 fathoms of water. As things turned out, this was to be heaven-sent for the 45 men out of 650 that were sailing in the Almiranta.

The priest's account described the tragedy that unfolded:

The Almiranta attempted to turn completely around. But as the currents were flowing towards the banks and she was rather long, she was doing this with great

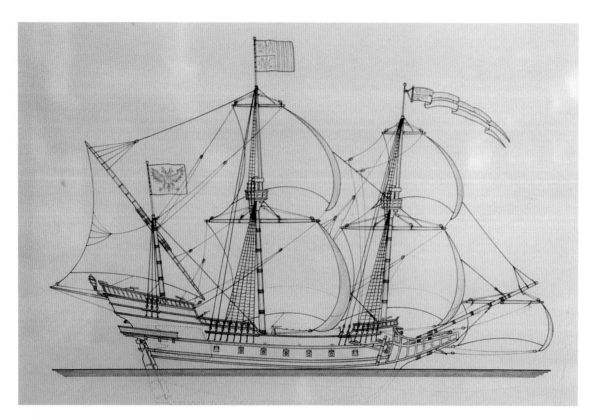

Galleon. Artist's depiction.

difficulty. The Capitana was a little ahead of the Almiranta. And as a more maneuverable ship, she turned around much more easily than the Almiranta. This set the Capitana on a collision course with the Almiranta. Because of the darkness of the night, they didn't see her until she was so close to us that had we changed our course to let her pass we would have surely rammed her. As such, our pilots ordered everyone to shout loudly to alert the Capitana of our position so that she could pass by us by our stern. Everyone shouted as ordered but to no avail. For the Capitana smashed against us by the washboard and her bowsprit went through the Almiranta from port to starboard. She gave such a blow to our boom that was on the collision side with her cutwater, which has been newly refitted in Havana and made of mahogany, that it broke in three pieces. This boom was seven palms thick. That blow broke through our planks from the top of the waterline to the holds, making splinters out of all of them.

The *Maravillas* was driven onto the banks and shoals. Instead of gently grounding, the vessel began to break apart. Father Rivadeneyra

A gold belt recovered from the *Maravillas*.

Close up of the gold belt showing one link.

described the aftermath of the collision. ". . . The ship began to touch bottom so roughly and to bump against the rocks so forcefully that her seams began to crack. The ship began to settle on the bottom. However, the waves grew and broke against the ship in such a way that they began to break some of the sides of plank into pieces."

The priest was hearing confessions, including the confession of Admiral Don Mathias de Orellana, "Who told me that we would surely die and that as such I should grant abso-

lution to everyone. I heard their confessions of sin and advised them to repent from them in order to obtain absolution."

The priest managed to stay afloat on a hatch cover until he was rescued by a launch from another galleon the next day.

SPANISH RECOVERY

Divers and six frigates were dispatched from Cuba after the *Jesus Maria* reached Havana and reported the wrecking. The site had been marked with buoys before the Spanish left— but they were not found by the salvors who had to drag for the ship.

While 480,000 pesos were recovered, four of the salvage boats were lost in a raging hurricane on June 19, 1656. Some of the treasure was later recovered from the sunken salvage boats.

Spanish archives record that salvage efforts in August of that year removed 650,000 pesos of treasure and some bronze cannons from what contemporary salvors concluded was the bow of the *Maravillas*.

The Spanish were relentless in their attempts to recover treasure from sunken galleons. It wasn't until 1677 and again in 1678 that Spanish salvors recorded removing three and a half tons of silver from the *Maravillas*.

MODERN SALVAGE

Almost three hundred years later, an enthusiastic diver who had been excavating the lost city of Port Royal in Jamaica began research in the Archives of the Indies in Seville. The young diver

Fork and spoon recovered from a Spanish galleon. Sailors had to supply their own utensils aboard ship.

found references to the *Maravillas* and its cargo manifest among the polilla worm–eaten records. It wasn't until eleven years after his initial research that Bob Marx found what he described as the bow of the *Maravillas* on May 24, 1972.

Marx's first piece of eight bore the date 1655. He was using a converted shrimp boat he named *Grifon*, after the one ship that escaped the hurricane of 1715 that claimed Captain-General Ubilla's fleet off the coast of Sebastian, Florida. That first day Marx found four gold coins and 1,720 silver coins along with many important artifacts from shipboard life.

Bob Marx had been very successful and resourceful but felt he—like the early Spanish salvors—had only found the bow section

of the elusive galleon. Controversy between Marx and the government of the Bahamas led to disagreements, and Marx left the site and was forbidden to return to continue his search and salvage of the *Maravillas*.

After Bob Marx was forced off the *Maravillas*, another treasure diver, Herbert Humphreys, negotiated with the Bahamas government and obtained a lease to search for the *Maravillas*. Humphreys knew that the treasure galleon shipped fifty-eight bronze cannons—and forty of them were still on the wreck site. Using one of the divers who worked with Bob Marx, Humphreys and his team located and worked the *Maravillas's* bow section in the Little Bahamas Bank area, north of Memory Rock.

Gold coins. When Mel Fisher first joined Kip Wagner working the 1715 fleet off Sebastian, he found the ocean floor carpeted with gold.

Humphreys's exploits found treasure, but hurricanes and ocean storms forced him to quit the site after his initial success finding gold and silver coins, uncut emeralds, and many ships accoutrements.

Humphreys didn't give up his search for the main part of the galleon, which would contain the bulk of the treasure. In 1987, he mounted another expedition aboard his vessel *Beacon* along with treasure hunter Art Hartman, who operated another salvage vessel called *The Dare*.

Using sophisticated search equipment that would detect the presence of ferrous metal underwater, Humphreys and Hartman and their crews began finding wreckage, and then uncut emeralds, along with coins and other objects.

That the exploration of the underwater area off Little Bahamas Bank yielded up a fortune in treasure is not disputed. What remains is the conclusion that millions more in gold, silver, and precious uncut gems have yet to be found. The *Maravillas* remains protected by Bahamian authorities. Someday its fortune in treasure will be recovered.

THE SHIPWRECK OFF JUPITER BEACH

Civilization flourished along the Loxahatchee River for thousands of years. Midden piles of shell and stone implements used by native people in the area have been carbon-dated to AD 750. Archaeological digs have revealed artifacts that were used by people who inhabited the land on this southeastern shore of Florida 10,000 years ago.

Ship in a gale. Artist's rendition in oil from the Bob and Margaret Weller collection. Used by permission.

Aerial view taken from a helicopter of the Jupiter Inlet showing the shipwreck site offshore just south of the inlet.

The area in the vicinity of what is today known as Jupiter is an amazing combination of estuary and mangroves with an inlet leading from the river to the ocean. At different times in history a natural cut meandered to the ocean. It was located south of its present position. Today, the Jupiter inlet is maintained by stone and cement jetties and sea walls, and dredging keeps the passageway clear for navigation.

Surely John Cabot came upon this land in 1496. The English followed on the heels of Columbus's discoveries and sought their own conquests in the New World. The Spaniard Juan Ponce de León, with a warrant from the crown, came upon this area of Florida on April 2, 1513. It was the day of celebration of *Pascua Florida*, the Passover Feast of Flowers, for which he then named the land.

Nineteen days later, Ponce de León found the river that led from the ocean to the interior. He called it Rio de la Cruz, planted a cross at its confluence, and claimed the land for the King of Spain. The river is now called the Loxahatchee.

Long before engineers cut an even channel through to the ocean, there was a natural but irregular channel perhaps a quarter- to a half-mile south of the present-day cut. Sailing into the cut, early explorers were startled by the abundance and beauty of the place.

Another aerial view of the Jupiter Inlet. Just south of the jetty off the public bathing beach is where life-guard Peter Leo discovered the shipwreck.

Native inhabitants regarded the area as a place of bounty where fish and shellfish could be caught and where there were plentiful supplies of fresh water.

The native people did not welcome the Spanish. Ponce de León's log, inspected by Spanish scholar Antonio de Herrera in 1592, described what happened when the explorer and his men ventured on shore:

(The Indians) . . . tried to steal the launch, the oars, and arms . . . they struck a seaman in the head with a club, from which he was

knocked out, they had to do battle with them, who with their arrows and armed shafts, the points of sharpened bones, and fish spines, wounded two Spaniards . . . He departed from there to a river where he took on water and firewood . . . Sixty Indians massed to harass him . . . He gave this river the name La Cruz and left at it a cross hewn from quarry stone . . .

This was Ponce de León's first and last attempt to navigate the Loxahatchee River and explore the area around present-day Jupiter.

The explorer was shot and killed by an Indian arrow eight years later on Florida's west coast.

The area of the Jupiter Inlet was called Ho Bay by the native people who built a fishing village there. The Spanish called it *Jobe*, and the English translated *Jobe* to *Jove*, since they assumed it was named for that god. It became Jupiter.

History overtook the quiet settlement of this part of Florida's east coast. The Spanish were mining silver in Peru. Mexico was conquered in 1519. Gold and emeralds, silver and pearls, spices and hides became the trafficked goods funneled back to Spain in ships of all kinds and dimensions.

Armadas of armed ships of the crown would escort merchant galleons along the coast off Jupiter in convoys. Small armed sloops—the Spanish called them pataches—avisos or courier ships, and various merchant vessels would supply Spain's Atlantic coastal Florida settlement in St. Augustine. These smaller vessels would make the trip from Havana, through the Bahama Channel along the coast of Florida with mail, supplies, and payment for the troops and cargo once St. Augustine was established in 1565.

Wars raged in Europe. Greed for division of the New World's wealth seethed as English, Dutch, French, Spanish, and Portuguese powers established colonies to exploit the wealth. When the Spanish Armada was defeated by the English in 1588, Spain was no longer the unchallenged master of the Ocean Sea and no longer safe in the waters of the Atlantic Ocean, Gulf of Mexico, Caribbean, or along the coast of Florida.

LIFEGUARD FINDS TREASURE

The coins reflected golden rays like mirrors in the sun. The gold doubloons were each struck by hand and minted in the New World by Spanish conquistadors using enslaved Indian labor. As the ocean lifeguard looked at the gold coins and gold bars, he reflected on the long journey that brought him to that moment—a moment many dream about, discovery of a shipwreck laden with treasure.

Peter Leo is a career ocean lifeguard. He was stationed on Jupiter Beach, one of the northernmost beaches in Palm Beach County, Florida, on the Atlantic Ocean. Peter wasn't a treasure hunter, but he had always spent time on the water with his family as a child. He sailed as a youth and became an accomplished boat handler and a licensed boat captain.

Peter found things in the ocean. He salvaged motors and parts of ships that wrecked after storms and were abandoned by their owners. His diving had been limited to snorkeling for pleasure and occasional scuba dives for fun, made on visits to see his cousin, a Navy commander in charge of the U.S. base on the island of Bermuda.

Peter knew of the great Spanish shipwreck finds made in Bermuda waters by his cousin's friend, legendary Bermudian Teddy Tucker. Peter wasn't thinking about Spanish treasure or shipwrecks on the morning that would change his life forever.

He came to work early on July 13, 1987, to get in his hour of routine physical conditioning before assuming his post in the lifeguard tower. Lifeguards work out every morning—rowing,

To locate a shipwreck salvors often followed the direction of the chain or direction of the anchor ring. The anchors were dropped over the side to keep the ship from going onto the reef. Hurricane-force winds parted the chain and cable and the ship would be forced back in the direction of the gale winds.

Peter Leo with the cannon underwater off Jupiter Beach. He first saw the cannon, dove down and decided to raise it. This led to the discovery of the remains of the shipwreck.

Peter Leo with gold recovered from the Jupiter wreck.

jogging on the beach, swimming. Peter decided to swim. He donned his fins and swim goggles and swam offshore, parallel to the beach.

The water was warm and clear. "I was looking at the bottom through my goggles," said Peter. "It was sand, sand, sand. I swam through a large school of baitfish. I looked down and saw a large dark object; took a breath and dove down. I saw a tremendous fluke of an anchor and knew it was old. I surfaced, caught a breath, and dove down again. Next to the anchor was an encrusted cannon."

Peter had worked as a lifeguard for the previous eleven years on Jupiter's public beach. He swam the same offshore area every day. He rescued bathers from the surf, rowed the beach patrol's pram, and used the inflatable to help boaters in distress. He snorkeled and knew the ocean area off his beach by heart.

When Peter discovered the anchor and cannon, it was sheer luck. Wind, waves, sea, and storm removed a blanket of sand that had covered them for centuries. "I had no idea of its age but knew one thing. I was going to raise that cannon," Peter said.

Peter went back to the lifeguard station and scratched his name and social security number on a piece of aluminum along with the legend, "FOUND." He swam back to the cannon and attached his small tag. Like Spanish explorers before him, Peter Leo claimed the cannon, not for Spain, but for himself.

It was clear that Peter and his fellow lifeguards couldn't bring up the cannon without winches and a barge. Peter obtained a barge from a nearby marina and began the adventure of a lifetime.

Peter and his friends got dive gear together. Calls to the state of Florida to obtain requisite permission to raise the cannon were fraught with delays. The state had no one to send to help. Knowing that any delay would put his find at risk, Peter and his group of friends went to work to raise the cannon.

"It took us all day to chip and hack the coral away from the cannon tube," Peter said. The cannon was encrusted with marine growth and attached to coral rock on the seabed. As the cannon was lifted free, an old Spanish copper bucket came up with it. The bucket, crushed under the cannon, convinced Peter that there was more to be found nearby.

The iron cannon weighed 960 pounds. It was a four-pounder, a cannon that would fire four-pound cannon balls. Peter and his friends decided to explore the area with a metal detector the next day. They discovered more cannons. In a recess in the coral base under the sand, the divers found their first piece of eight. The coin was struck in Potosi, now part of Bolivia, formerly part of the Spanish viceroyalty of Peru. The coin was dated 1658.

Peter called Mel Fisher's office in Key West. Fisher was a legend, having already discovered the *Atocha* and *Santa Margarita*. Jim Sinclair, Mel's archaeologist, advised Peter and his group to hire a lawyer. The young explorers obtained the name of a lawyer, David Horan, the man who successfully protected Mel Fisher's finds in federal admiralty court.

"We filed an admiralty claim in U.S. District Court," Peter explained. This was only the beginning of a process required to claim possession and salvage rights to the shipwreck he discovered. The admiralty claim was complicated by the fact that the very spot where Peter discovered the cannon was designated a beach renourishment project site.

The plan was to dump tons of sand from nearby Jupiter Inlet on the beach and ocean area where he made his find. The same storms that uncovered the cannon and anchor, which made the discovery possible, took sand off the

Diver Debbie Pawlak snorkeling down to inspect the Jupiter shipwreck cannons.

The crushed copper bucket found by Peter Leo under the first cannon he removed from the Jupiter shipwreck site.

public swimming beach. Authorities wanted to put the sand back.

The state of Florida entered the court action to protect the find and ensure the excavation of the site would preserve the historical and archaeological information and artifacts.

The U.S. District Court granted custodianship over the wreck site to the divers. They formed a small corporation to exploit the find. Agreement was reached with the state. The divers promised to employ proper techniques for the excavation, conservation, and recording of artifacts. The state was given the right to any unique artifact discovered and a 20-percent share in the finds.

Peter worked to make progress before the beach renourishment project began. He dove on the site on his days off and his vacation days. "We were only allowed to fan the sand away by hand the entire first three summers," Peter said. "We submitted reports and came up with archaeological research and plans that would satisfy the state of Florida." Even by fanning the sand away by hand, the divers found a thousand pieces of eight.

Each coin offered a clue to the shipwreck. The cob coins—clipped from the end of a bar of silver, which had been poured into sand and clay, hammered flat, then struck with dies at mints in the New World—bore mint and assayer marks. In some cases, there were legible dates on the coins. The shield of the Spanish monarchy also helped date coins that had no legible dates.

Silver pieces of eight attached to coral as they were found on the shipwreck site.

In those first months, the divers found no provenance—nothing that enabled them to identify the ship they were working. The area of the find was in shallow water, about eleven feet deep, only a hundred yards off Jupiter Beach.

CLUES OF THE COINS

Coins the divers brought up from the site bore dates between 1652 and 1659. Mint marks were from Potosi, Lima, Mexico City, and Bogota. "The thing we found the most of were coins," Peter said. "Mostly silver eight reales with Potosi mint marks dated 1658. Some were heavily deteriorated, but others were in good shape, depending on where they lay for the last few centuries. If they were near iron objects, such as the cannons, the coins were in excellent condition since the iron prevented oxidation of the silver," Peter said.

The divers worked closely with archaeologists to discover origin and identity of the shipwreck. No coins were found with dates after 1659. The team concluded that the ship wrecked in 1659 or early 1660. From numismatic experts Peter learned that a coin dated 1659 and minted in Lima could only have been made around the time of the wrecking.

A silver piece of eight from the Jupiter wreck.

Author on the Jupiter shipwreck site with gold below.

"The mint was opened and closed in that same year. It was opened by the Viceroy of Peru, Count Alba de Liste [also spelled in historical accounts as Aliste] without authorization from the King of Spain. When the king found out, he ordered the mint shut down and the dies destroyed. Very few coins bearing that date and mint mark are known to exist," Peter said. Scarce 1659 Lima pieces of eight in good condition are worth an estimated $25,000 each to collectors.

The Lima Star was the first piece of eight of that variety that the state of Florida had ob- tained from shipwreck sites under its jurisdiction. Since the coins only appeared in 1659 and for a short period in 1660, they were virtually unknown among collectors. The Lima Star coins were stamped "LIMA" under a shooting star with eight points. The coins are dated 1659 and bear the Spanish assayer's initial V for Villegas.

The amazing part of Spanish colonial coinage is that every coin is different. Mint markings described history by using symbolic designs on their dies. The city of Lima had been considered the City of Three Kings by

Pieces of eight.

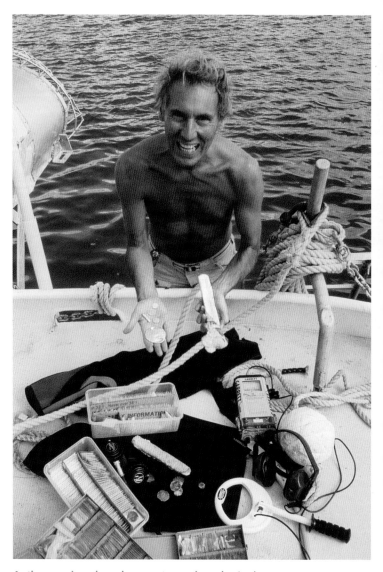

Author coming aboard support vessel on the Jupiter shipwreck site with some of the treasure found below.

the colonists. Thus, when the brief coinage was initiated and the Lima mint reopened—because coins were in short supply—the Star of Bethlehem was stamped on the coins between the Pillars of Hercules.

A gold puddle or disk was found, along with small finger bars of gold. The puddle was pure gold. It weighed about eight ounces and had been poured into a sand or clay mold. There were no markings on the gold puddle or on the gold finger bars, and no royal tax stamps.

Spain taxed treasure 20 percent, and assayers marked and stamped bars to denote that they were declared and the tax was paid. These

Gold coins, silver pieces of eight, disks, and finger bars of gold from the Jupiter shipwreck.

finger bars and the gold puddle were being smuggled, so the owners could avoid paying the Royal Fifth to the king's tax collectors.

The divers discovered a large silver bar. They hoped the numbers and stamps on the bar would aid in identifying the shipwreck. The Spanish kept careful records of all treasure that was loaded aboard ships from the New World.

The silver bar was made in 1652. It bore the monogram of King Philip IV, and the weight of the ingot was stamped as 154 marks plus one. This meant the bar weighed seventy-seven pounds of silver plus one pound of alloy. It was common that alloys in early silver were copper or tin; but also, since it had no value at the time, many silver bars were alloyed with platinum.

A chunk had been taken out of the silver bar, which was the assayer's bite, the portion used to test silver purity and also the fee for the service.

Gold coins from the Jupiter shipwreck.

A silver coin after cleaning in electrolytic bath to remove corrosion.

Dr. Eugene Lyon was consulted. Unlike Mel Fisher's legendary silver bars that correlated with the *Atocha's* manifest discovered by Dr. Lyon in the Spanish archives, the information Jupiter wreck divers were able to provide Dr. Lyon did not enable him to decipher what shipwreck it was from.

"As a historical researcher working on this site for the salvors, I have examined the silver ingot, several silver and gold coins, and other artifacts recovered from the site. My goal on the project is to realize a definitive identification of the wreck site through primary archival documents and their correlation with site data. First, there seems to be little doubt that the site is Spanish colonial in nature. Coin dating, cannon size, and the ingot are the best evidence offered to date, the coins indicating a site with a 'terminus post quem' after 1658," Dr. Eugene Lyon wrote in a letter to Carl Clausen, Florida's consulting archaeologist dated December 19, 1988.

Working on the assumption that the Jupiter shipwreck was a lone vessel, Dr. Lyon wrote:

The bar was stamped with its value, 8012 reales of silver and 1683 of copper. Another stamp in Roman numerals, DCCCXX, a tally number from the mint, revealed that the bar was the 820th ingot cast that year in the royal foundry. The high alloy content required the bar to be stamped with devaluation marks by the assayer. The bar's value was 812 pesos 1683 *maravedies*, or 2255 silver out of 2400—below the assayer's requirements for purity.

The avisos were small vessels. Seven that the House of Trade contracted to be built in 1628 were 50–60 toneladas [tons] in displacement. These proved, however, too small for the voyage and, in 1649, it was provided that the Vera Cruz avisos should not exceed 100 toneladas. At times the couriers carried cargo, but usually were officially limited to carrying the governmental and

Earl Young preparing a Jupiter shipwreck cannon in an electrolytic bath.

religious correspondence—Viceregal reports, Treasury accounts and audits, legal cases and court decisions, residencies, probate accounts, etc. There always existed, however, the possibility of illicit ladings aboard the avisos. Contraband cargoes were carried throughout the colonial epoch . . . Also the ships carried funds for supplies and payroll.

In the end, the man who was able to offer proof positive that Mel Fisher had indeed discovered the wreck of the *Atocha* by correlating silver bars recovered underwater with numbers and weights listed on the ship's manifest, concluded about the Jupiter wreck: "I have examined the silver ingot recovered from the site . . . Despite the salvor's natural interest in the ingot, it cannot presently serve as a useful tool in the definitive identification of the shipwreck, for it exists in isolation."

Peter Leo did not find a Spanish galleon. Archive records did not support the wrecking of a galleon upon Jupiter's shores; however, two avisos were known to have wrecked off modern-day Jupiter.

Was the treasure from a galleon that wrecked elsewhere? Was it a ship that broke apart in a storm and part of a shipwreck that was tossed by hurricane-force winds and waves onto the shores of Jupiter—where its wood was consumed by worms and its heavy cargo settled under the sand off the beach, only to be found years later as the sands shifted with ocean storms? Was the shipwreck a solitary vessel, a *suelto*, sailing on a mission; an aviso, or courier ship heading, from Cuba to St. Augustine? The silver bar was only one piece in a puzzle Peter hoped to solve with the excavation.

Earl Young, a Coast Guardsman assigned to the Jupiter Lighthouse Station and later to the USCG station on Peanut Island in West Palm Beach, had just signed up for a scuba course. "It was a month later that Peter found the cannon," Earl said.

Divers Larry Bain (in hat) and Earl Young working the hookah rig, a compressor that supplies air to divers working below, on the Jupiter shipwreck site.

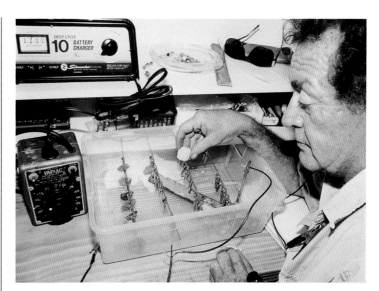

A conservationist preparing a coin for cleaning in an electrolytic bath.

"I had vacation coming from the Coast Guard. I took my leave and went diving on the shipwreck just about every day. The first weeks were pretty hectic," Earl said. "We were calling everywhere. It was a learning experience."

Earl Young had to learn conservation techniques to prevent the cannon and other artifacts being brought up from disintegrating when the salt on them dried and crystallized. Artifacts first had to be bathed in fresh water, then treated in electrolytic baths to rid them of centuries-old salt crystals that would shatter the iron if left to dry on land.

Peter hoped to put the cannons and anchors from the wreck on display in Jupiter and create displays in the local history museum of the finds recovered from the shipwreck. Earl was beginning the long process of stabilizing the iron.

Earl explained how he did it. "We put a charge into the artifacts themselves and attached the positive pole to a piece of stainless steel in the bath. The steel serves as the anode—the positive pole; the anode will draw the impurities out of the artifacts," he said.

Electrolytic baths for large iron artifacts require a lot of time, perhaps as long as three years for cannons. The same process is used to

The Jupiter shipwreck dive team preparing artifacts for an electrolytic bath to preserve them.

remove oxidation from silver coins. The process for small or fragile artifacts is carefully monitored and the electric current is reduced, since it may only require an hour or two to clean corroded silver coins.

The effect of leaving iron artifacts, removed from salt water, without treatment is evident to any visitor to the Florida Keys. Cannons and galleon anchors taken from shipwrecks in the early days of salvage are used to decorate the fronts of hotels, restaurants, and dive shops—and they have crumbled apart as the salt and impurities crystallize.

"Nothing harms gold coins or bars. Gold comes up basically encrustation-free without being affected by seawater. The problem with gold is when it is not completely pure. Spanish refining methods didn't get all the alloys out of the gold, so some of the bars and coins have encrustations on them," Earl said.

As excavation of the Jupiter wreck progressed, Peter began to recognize that they were not finding parts of the ship itself. "There should be a lot more spikes, belt buckles, pottery, ballast stones, iron tools. Things we've not found but should find here," Peter said.

"It could be just a hundred yards away. Perhaps this part of the ship broke off. We've probably recovered a portion of the middle or upper deck of the boat," Peter reflected. "We're missing olive jars, tools, and the personal gear that is usually down in the lower part of a Spanish ship. These objects sit more in a pile. Mostly we have scattered coins, which would have been stored in the upper part of the ship," he added.

The scatter pattern was an important problem the team was trying to solve. It appeared that the wreckage was spread over a large area of ocean. Sophisticated search and recovery equipment was necessary to locate more wreckage under ten to fifteen feet of sand. The team consulted experts who fitted out a search boat with magnetometers (or mags), side-scan sonar, and computerized ship-positioning equipment.

The plan was that each *hit*, or magnetometer reaction, to an anomaly below could be

A diver with a treasure detector working the shipwreck site.

Peter Leo (front left), famed Bermuda shipwreck diver Teddy Tucker (center front), his daughter Wendy Tucker, and the author (back) with Jupiter shipwreck coins.

plotted on the computer. It was then logged for a future search, without the need to stop the search boat each time to mark the spot so divers could return to it later.

A radio-positioning station was established on a post on Jupiter Beach. The team had already put up visual markers on land so they could take readings with a sextant. By measuring angles with the sextant they could plot the exact position of their workboat and keep a log of where they dug holes in the sand with the ship's blowers or mailboxes and where they found artifacts.

The team could use this information to make an archaeological map of the site. A radio beacon, attached to the post on shore, sent signals to the search boat. The search boat's radio receiver was hooked into a portable computer. As Peter drove the search boat over the site, operators worked the locating receivers. Anomalies were recorded on the computer, which would also enter the position.

Magnetometers were pulled behind the search boat. The only thing a mag will detect is iron or ferrous metal. The problem the searchers faced, in the area just north and south of the Jupiter Inlet, was that it was a veritable underwater junkyard. Scrap of all

Diver Larry Bain with coins from the Jupiter shipwreck that he found below with a metal detector.

The sonar recorder has a graph, and the object is outlined on a chart. The amount of junk on the bottom, buried under Jupiter's shifting sand, continued to be a problem even with the most sophisticated equipment.

TREASURE RECOVERY

Once the state of Florida gave permission to use blowers to excavate the site, Peter set to work. He chartered the *Miss Eula*, a forty-foot converted steel tug with twin 871 Detroit diesel engines that belonged to a friend, Bermuda treasure diver Teddy Tucker. This workboat proved to be just what the team needed to excavate the site.

The ship was equipped with twin prop deflectors, elbow-shaped mailboxes that could be lowered over the ship's large propellers. *Miss Eula's* large props and the powerful diesel engines enabled the team to dig holes down through the sand and expose bedrock below, where the artifacts had settled.

As soon as *Miss Eula* was brought onto the site with its onboard compressor, a hookah rig that supplied divers working below with air through long hoses connected to the compressor, the team began finding artifacts. Once the blowers cleared sand away and dug a hole, divers below used handheld metal detectors and searched exposed recesses in coral rocks.

There were thousands of sinkers, lost over the years by fishermen in the area. The divers accumulated the sinkers in a large pail along with other trash. Some days only a few silver coins were found; on lucky days several

Diver Larry Bain surfacing with coins found on the Jupiter shipwreck site.

kinds—discarded dredge pipes, engine blocks, and modern debris—produced readings.

The divers tried using side-scan sonar. More sophisticated than magnetometers, side-scan sonar sends out sound waves that are reflected back as echoes once they strike something underwater, even under sand covering an object buried on the bottom.

Fragments of human skull found on the Jupiter shipwreck site.

hundred silver pieces of eight were found in a few hours.

Peter began discovering unusual artifacts. A small pewter box with tiny holes in the lid turned out to be a shaker for fine sand that would be sprinkled over ink to make it dry.

Diver Larry Bain, working under the mailbox, found small pieces of human bone. Larry showed the bone fragments to team member Debbie Pawlak who recognized them as part of a human skull. Debbie contacted Dr. Maurice Thomas, professor of Human Anatomy and Physiology at Palm Beach Atlantic College, to help identify the bone fragments. Dr. Thomas visited the site and brought with him anatomical models of human skulls to compare with the finds.

"You can see how these sutures fit the bone together," Dr. Thomas explained. He turned the shipwreck-site bone fragments over in his hands, then carefully placed them together at the suture lines where the skull is joined together.

"This looks like a suture line. You can see the thickness corresponds pretty well. If you look at the inside, there's a little groove that

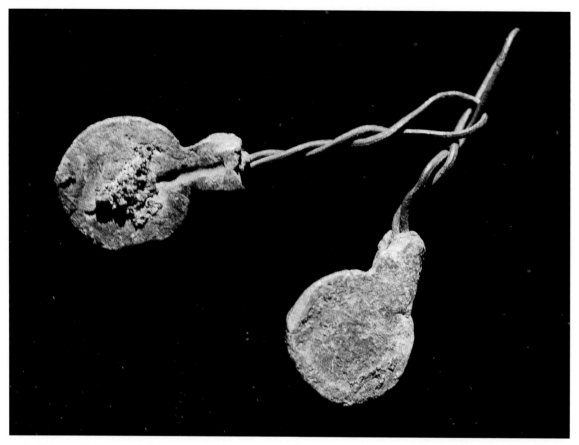

Split shot was loaded into blunderbusses or cannons and fired at enemy ships. The shot decimated sailors on deck and tore sails apart.

corresponds," Dr. Thomas said. The anatomy professor fit the shipwreck skull into the cutaway anatomical model. The pieces fit perfectly, and Dr. Thomas skillfully joined the fragments of bone together so they matched.

The Jupiter shipwreck presented more mysteries than answers. Who was this hapless victim of the tragic sinking? The historical context of the period was the end of the Thirty Years' War that had raged in Europe from 1618 to 1648. No Spanish treasure convoy sailed in 1659 or 1660 from the New World. Sueltos, or single ships, were plying the waters from Ha-

vana back to Spain, and many avisos or courier ships were taking mail and documents to St. Augustine and Spain. Still there was no definitive answer to identify the shipwreck.

The U.S. Army Corps of Engineers put a temporary moratorium on the dumping of dredged sand from Jupiter Inlet onto the shipwreck site. Hurricanes and ocean storms continued to erode Jupiter's bathing beach. A project was undertaken to pump sand from the inlet onto the beach near the jetty. Peter and his team of divers were working just offshore, so the site became covered with sandy silt and

Peter Leo with gold bars, one with silver pieces of eight attached to it—treasure from the Jupiter shipwreck.

visibility was reduced. The divers could hardly see their hands underwater.

The small team continued to work, returning each morning with *Miss Eula*. They blew holes down through the sand with the prop deflectors until they reached bedrock and the limestone base.

Security was not a problem on the site. Many snorkelers swam out from the beach to watch the divers and to look at the cannons and anchors the team uncovered. Since blowers would have to be used to move the ten feet of sand that sat on top of the wreckage, any illegal activity during the day would be seen by Jupiter lifeguards who worked with Peter.

By night, Palm Beach County Sheriff's deputies patrolled the park and beach area. The shipwreck site was just a stone's throw from the beach. Unlike the sites of the *Atocha* and *Santa Margarita*, located far from land off Key West, Peter's shipwreck was in a location that afforded perfect security. The deep shifting sands, however, covered the site—making it necessary to continuously blow holes to get down to bedrock.

The main pile of ballast stones has not been located. Old aerial photographs that Peter obtained of the area revealed that the place where he first found the cannon and anchor, just south of the Jupiter Inlet, had all been beach at one time. Sunbathers spread their beach umbrellas and towels over the treasure buried deep beneath the sand.

Over the centuries—with storms, tidal action, and ocean waves—Jupiter's natural inlet, located south of the present-day man-

made cut from the Loxahatchee River and Intracoastal Waterway to the Atlantic Ocean, had shifted. It was evidence of geological changes to the ocean area where the shipwreck was located.

"We found eleven cannons and two anchors with nine-foot shanks. The cannons were small four- and six-pounders," Peter said. "This led us to conclude that we had a medium-sized vessel, not a galleon," he said.

Some cannon balls the divers recovered were grenade types, others were bar shot, two rounded ends connected by an iron bar, designed to take down an enemy ship's sails and rigging. The grenades had holes in them plugged with wood. They were filled with gunpowder. Arquebus guns, or early muskets, were brought up. X-rays revealed there was a musket ball inside one gun. That meant it was loaded and ready for action when the ship went down.

As Peter Leo and the team continued their excavation of the site in cooperation with the state of Florida, expenses continued to mount. State rules prohibited the sale of any coins or other artifacts until the state examined them, chose the artifacts they wanted for the museum in Tallahassee, and made a division with the salvors. Just as things were getting strapped financially, a diver found two gold bars.

The gold bars weighed approximately four pounds each, were about ten inches long, and were encrusted with silver pieces of eight. One bar had four coins attached to it, the other six coins. There were no official Spanish mint marks on the gold and no official assayer's marks, which led to the inevitable conclusion that the gold was contraband being smuggled by its owners. These gold bars, like the eight-ounce puddle and the finger bars, were contraband.

The discovery of the gold sent waves of excitement through the team. They searched and re-searched the area where the gold bars were found. No more were found, and the divers returned to their routine—searching systematically over the grid pattern they had established.

Archive research was continuing in Seville. A letter was discovered that mentioned a Spanish aviso. The letter was from the governor of Cartagena to the president of the Council of the Indies and was dated April 25, 1660. The letter related: "The aviso that sailed from Cartagena on September 18, 1659, the one that was sent by the Count de Alba, Viceroy of Peru, under the care of Juan Ramirez de Miranda . . . has not arrived . . . and is believed to be lost. She was the *San Miguel*, the owner and master was Juan de Ortolara."

Researcher Robert Stenuit, who found the letter in the Archive of the Indies in Seville, discovered a notation on the back that read, "We are already informed of the loss of the ship of Juan Ramirez de Miranda."

Stenuit found testimony among the archives that described the ship by name as *San Miguel Archangel* captained by Juan de Ortolara and piloted by Diego Garcia. The documents described what the vessel was carrying.

Stenuit translated the document: "One small chest marked 'To The King,' size 42cm x

30 x 30 which was protected by green waxed cloth and carefully nailed and again, protected by a second exterior plain bramante [a type of strong cloth from Peru]. The same messenger was carrying additionally, another small chest . . . as well as two other small chests from the President of Española and various other bunches of letters."

The aviso *San Miguel Archangel* left Porto Bello on July 25, 1659, carrying Captain Juan Ramirez de Miranda to Cartagena. On September 18, 1659, the records revealed that the *San Miguel* sailed from Cartagena for Spain. Stenuit was able to confirm that the aviso actually sailed when he discovered a letter that read, "I have written last to Your Majesty in April by the aviso of courier Juan Ramirez de Miranda."

Circumstantial evidence about the shipwreck coincided with historical facts about the striking of silver pieces of eight at the Lima mint in 1659. These coins could not have left Callao, a seaport town in Peru near Lima, before April 1659. The archives revealed that no ships sailed between the end of January and April.

Archive records searched by Robert Stenuit revealed, by process of elimination, that the Jupiter wreck could not have been a warship since the dates provided by the coins recovered coincided with time periods when no ships were lost from any fleet.

No fleet sailed in 1659 or 1660 because of the menace from Spain's enemy, England. The July 1661 fleet that sailed from Havana lost no ships. No fleet sailed from Tierra Firme in

1662. The flota of 1663 returned to Spain without losing any ships.

During this period Spanish shipping was menaced by British men-of-war and privateers sailing the Caribbean from their stronghold on the island of Jamaica. To evade detection and capture, the Spanish used fast, well-armed avisos to carry official mail and dispatches along with passengers returning to Spain.

Records from the archives revealed that the *San Miguel Archangel* wrecked near a place the Spanish called Xega, Jegay, or Jega. The name was spelled in different ways, but it meant the area around today's Jupiter. Other archive documents described a Spanish boat coming from South America that wrecked on the coast of Jega.

The records revealed that there were thirty-three survivors of the shipwreck. A ship was sent south from St. Augustine to rescue them. One reference mentions that local Indians stripped the survivors of their clothes and belongings. No record was found in Spanish archives of any attempt to salvage the *San Miguel Archangel* at the time of its sinking.

The scatter pattern of the Jupiter wreck appears to be in an east-northeast direction from the place of the first discovery just south of the Jupiter Inlet jetty. When Peter plotted the location of the cannons on a map, the first cannon and anchor were almost directly in line with the two other cannons located about fifty feet farther south from the first two.

Almost in line, some twenty-three feet from the two cannons, closer to the beach, were three more cannons and an anchor. The layout resembled a diamond—with the original cannon find at the northern top, cannons at each point, and two cannons in the middle of the diamond.

The location of coins and artifacts were plotted where they were found in relation to the cannons and anchors. This plotting offered no proof about the scatter line. A storm at sea would have tossed the aviso like a matchbox. Avisos were small, fast ships and mounted from ten to twenty cannons for defense.

THE QUEST CONTINUES

Today, Peter Leo and his small team of divers continue their quest for more evidence. Perhaps an artifact will indeed confirm absolutely that the shipwreck they are excavating is the *San Miguel Archangel*.

Six thousand artifacts have been brought up and are being conserved. About 4,000 coins have been recovered. The state of Florida has granted divisions with the divers returning a share of the coins to them. It is as Mel Fisher once said, "It takes a lot of silver to find gold." A lot of treasure has come up, but Peter has yet to recover all his costs.

Many artifacts have been placed in the local historical society museum. Peter arranged for permanent display of two cannons and an anchor that were stabilized in Florida's archaeology laboratory in Tallahassee. The anchor and cannons are on the grounds of the Jupiter Lighthouse just off Highway A1A. They can

Sounding weights on top of a dead eye. The dead eye is made of lignum vitae wood. It was the equivalent of an ancient sailing ship's turnbuckle. Rigging was passed through the holes in the dead eye and secured. The sounding weights were recovered from the Corrigan's shipwreck site.

be viewed and enjoyed by visitors to the area. A bronze plaque describes the history of the shipwreck.

A lead cannon shield was found that bore the date 1659, and while Peter said, "There is no conclusion. We are still looking and finding," one thing is clear: local history is being discovered at this underwater site that was once the province of sunbathers and found by chance by an ocean lifeguard. 🚢

THE *San Jose*: RICHEST SHIPWRECK IN THE WORLD

here have been legendary shipwrecks, some with fabulous treasure aboard. None of those shipwrecks had as much treasure as the San Jose, *which was lost in a naval conflict off Cartagena, Colombia, in 1708.*

Fused mass of musket balls from sunken Spanish galleon of the 1715 fleet.

"When *Life* magazine came out with an article some years ago about the ten richest unrecovered treasures of the world on land or sea, the *San Jose* was number one. The *Atocha* was number seven and the *Central America* number eight," Bob Weller said. A smile crossed his face.

"The archives in Cartagena revealed that [the *San Jose*] had 55,000 gold eight escudos on board. Each is worth $7,500 today plus many silver bars and silver coins plus the personal wealth of some six hundred passengers.

"By today's value there is an estimated seven billion dollars on the bottom, making it the largest treasure trove, land or sea, still unrecovered," Weller continued.

"I can put my finger right on the wreck of the *San Jose*," he said. We were alone in the office in Weller's home in Lake Worth, Florida. The walls were decorated with a fortune in Spanish silver and artifacts Bob and his wife Margaret recovered from galleons along the Spanish Main.

His desk and shelves bulged with research documents and Spanish legajos, translations of the meticulous records kept by Spain's House of Trade in Seville.

Not too far away, tied at dockside farther up the coast, was the *Expedition*, a thirty-seven-foot Striker-made aluminum-hulled research vessel the Wellers fitted out to search for the *San Jose*.

When Bob Weller, dean of the worldwide salvage community that comprised many living legends of international acclaim, said he knew where a shipwreck was located, everyone listened.

By 1708, the Spanish convoy system to the New World functioned well. War with England raged and Spanish ships on the high seas were subject to attack.

Fortunes were to be made by the capture of treasure-laden Spanish ships. In 1708, Sir

Charles Wager, commander of four English ships, stationed his squadron at the mouth of Cartagena harbor to wait.

"All Commodore Wager wanted to do was capture a treasure galleon. The captain got 15 percent of the prize. He'd be rich for the rest of his life. Wager wrote that in a letter to a friend. He laid in wait in front of Cartagena in April 1708, with four ships."

"The *Expedition*, which was Wager's flagship, the *Portland*, the *Kingston*, and the *Vulture*. The *Vulture* was only a fire ship. They would set it on fire and run it into the enemy; there were no cannons aboard," Weller related.

Weller studied events involving the *San Jose* for many years. "Commodore Wager was on station patrolling in front of Cartagena harbor a better part of two months. The Spanish Tierra Firme Fleet under the command of Admiral Don Miguel Augustin de Villanueva had three primary galleons."

The Capitana was the *San Jose*; the Almiranta was officially the *San Joachin*. Another in the fleet was the *Santa Cruz*. The three ships had all the treasure aboard.

"Then an interesting thing happened. The Spanish fleet went into Porto Bello early in the year. While there, the Admiral on the *Santa Cruz* feuded with the captain-general in charge, Villanueva. As a result, Villanueva took all the treasure off the admiral's ship and put it aboard the Capitana and Almiranta."

"The ship Commodore Wager captured later on was the *Santa Cruz*. There was no treasure aboard, maybe thirteen bars of silver," Weller said.

The incident Weller related, a fateful event in maritime history, had been shaped by an argument between Spanish officers.

"While in Porto Bello, a Swedish ship came in and advised the Spanish that the English were lying off the port of Cartagena. A meeting of ship's captains and merchants was called. Even a notice was posted of the English threat. The captains were told that the British were lying in wait," Weller related.

"The majority said wait in Porto Bello. Villanueva said no. His words were: 'The sea is wide and its courses diverse. We'll sail in a couple of days.' He didn't feel the English were a real threat. He had fourteen armed ships. They sailed west out of Porto Bello to Cartagena," Weller said as he described the 1708 Tierra Firme Fleet's fateful voyage.

Logs of the British vessels on station describe the action. In 1708 the Spanish used the Gregorian calendar adopted by Pope Gregory while the British used the Julian calendar. This accounts for the ten day difference in dates of the battle described in the ships' logs. The entry for May 28, 1708, for the HMS *Expedition* reads:

Mother de la Popa* bore E ½ S. The little Brue** bore SSE 4 leagues. Thick heavy weather in the morning then clear and

---

*Mother de la Popa was the name of a large hill, above Cartagena Harbor visible from sea as a landmark.

**Little Brue (also spelled Brew and even Baru in the logs) was the name of the island off the coast of Cartagena.

moderate gales all this morning. Mother La Popa bore E 6 leagues and Little Brue SSE at 9 O'clock. Before noon we see 9 sails bearing of us S by W. At 10 see 10 sailes. At 12 noon see 17 sails. We then gave chase. Our Commodore shortening no sail till he was aboard the Admiral which was ahead and to windward of the Spanish galleon fleet, wearing a pennant at the top mast-head. About 6 at night we had the little Brue E by S of us 2 leagues. Our Commodore called to the Kingston *to engage the Vice Admiral. Their fleet consisted of 17 sail. An Admiral of 64 brass guns, carrying 600 men, a Vice Admiral carried 60 brass guns and 500 men, and a Rear Admiral 44 brass guns and 300 men. Of the fleet was 2 sloops and brigantine. He formed line of battleships a half hour past 6 we engaged the Admiral. After we had pass 6 broadsides she blew up. We had then 5 of their fleet engage us and no assistance of the other two being too far to windward. At 10 being dark we could not see none of his Admiral blowing up, they all separated but the rear Admiral his foretop mast or foretop sail. We gave him chase continued engagement with him all night. In this time the* Portland *came down but was so far to windward.*

Despite the terse old English log entry, the *Expedition's* position and the engagement are well described. The *San Jose* blew up.

THE BATTLE

The *Expedition's* log for May 29, continued:

Wind NE to NNW Little Brue ESE 7 leagues. Fair weather modest gales. We continued engaging the Rear Admiral till 3 O'clock this morning at which time seeing his ship so much disabled and now 3 ships against him he called for quarter which we granted. We had some men killed outright, 2 men who had their arms shot off and died of their wounds, and several wounded. Our sailes and rigging shot to pieces. We bent other sailes, knotted and spliced our rigging. At 6 this morning see 4 sailes to eastward. Made a signal to the Kingston *and* Portland *to chase. We lay by all night by the prize.*

The log of HMS *Portland* described the events and their position on May 28, 1708 as follows:

At 10 in the morning ye Little Brew S by E 4 leagues. These 24 hours small winds, all the afternoon hazy but all the rest of the time faire. This morning about nine of the clock made the Spanish fleet from the mast head containing 15 saile bearing S. These 24 hours faire weather all the afternoon, fresh gales but the rest of the time little wind, sometimes calm. 12 saile of the ships

Log of the *Expedition*.

laid by for us with their heads to ye Northward and between 6 and 7 of the clock at night began to engage, and in ye 2nd broadside ye Admiral of the Galleons gave ye Commodore* she blew up and ye fleet scattered. Soon after ye Commodore came up to us who had been engaged with a 32 gun French ship and one of ye Spanish on ye Reare Admiral quarter and at the same time had ye Reare Admiral of ye galleones on our luff on ye larboard side and ye Vice Admiral coming close to us standing to ye Southward we past our broadsides at each

other and kept on my way. Within a quarter of an hour after gave ye Reare Admiral our broadside and passed him. Ye Commodore having done ye like us then having sight of no more ships we all engaged ye ship passing [this was the Spanish Rear Admiral] and repassing him at 2 in the morning called out to us for quarter, being just going to fire into her at which time ye Commodore tack and sent his boat this morning.

*Wager was the commodore. Log entries refer to his ship, the *Expedition*, as ye Commodore.

Log of the *Portland*.

At daylight ye Kingston *signal and mine was out for chasing and I forthwith made what saile I could in ye engagement. Ye jolly boat was shot and sunk a stern, and our sails and rigging much disabled.*

The next entry in the *Portland's* log was for May 30, which gave the ship's position as "NW wind Noon Little Brew SE 5 leagues."

One of the Spanish ships ran into Little Brue (Baru) Island to escape the British. Spotted by the English, the Spanish ship ran aground onto the beach and was deliberately burned.

The log of HMS *Portland* described the event:

June 1 Wind variable. These 24 hours small winds sometimes calm and hazy. In the night much lightning. At 4 yesterday afternoon the ship finding she could not get from us run ashore under the Great Brew and set her on fire. Being a large ship and but 40 guns. At 7 at night we anchored about 2 miles from her in 30 fathoms water where she burnt all night...

Bob Weller described the geography of the islands lying off Cartagena harbor. "There are three major islands off Cartagena. Little Baru marked on contemporary charts as Isla del Rosario, Big Baru now known as Isla Grande on the charts, and Isla Tesoro.

"The Spanish fleet reached the eastern end of Little Baru at five or six at night and didn't have enough time in daylight to get into the harbor of Cartagena," Weller explained.

"The Spanish ships dropped sails and spent the night behind Little Brue. The thought was that in the morning when heat rises, the breeze would pull them landward and they would use that wind to get them into Cartagena. At 6 a.m. they'd try to make it around Little Brue about fifteen miles to Cartagena," Weller said.

"I've been there. But this morning the wind didn't develop. The English saw them about noontime. There was no wind. The only wind was in favor of the English who were about twenty miles away. They headed for the Spanish fleet. The Spanish thought they could make a turn around Isla de Tesoro and within ten miles be within the protection of the guns of the fort at the entrance to Cartagena. The wind just wasn't there," Weller explained.

"The English were able to close the distance so at six at night they took bearings on Tesoro and estimated the distance. The Spanish couldn't make it to the safety of Cartagena so formed a line of battle to the north. The British came alongside, and Commodore Wager engaged the Capitana, the *San Jose*. The HMS *Kingston* engaged the Almirante. In line of battle there was the Gobierno, Capitana, and Almirante.

"The line of battle was a half- to three-quarters of a mile long. The British came in and did a turn to the north and the firefight started," Weller said.

As Weller described the battle, the scene came alive with vivid descriptions he gleaned from the various ships' logs and contemporary accounts.

"The Almirante of the Spanish fleet took some pretty good hits and gave some pretty good hits. The *Portland* never had the stomach for the fight to begin with and never entered the battle until later that night. By 7 p.m. the sun had gone down. It was dark," Weller said.

"A cannon shot from the *Expedition* hit the *San Jose* and she blew up. The *San Jose* did not blow up in the air; she blew out her sides and sank with everything inside the hull," Weller said, using his hands for emphasis.

Commodore Sir Charles Wager's journal described the sinking of the *San Jose*:

May 29th—Calm till 3 o'clock yesterday then a small gale sprung up at NNE. Gave chase to the Galleons without hopes of being near them before night, but they finding they could not weather the Brue tacked and stood to northward with an easy sail, not endeavoring to go from us, but drawing into a sort of line of battle. The Admiral having a white or Spanish pendant at his main top mast in the center, the Vice Admiral the same pendant at

the fore mast head in the rear, and the Rear Admiral the same pendant at the mizzen top mast head in the van, about half a mile from one another and other ships in between them. Of the 17 sail, two were sloops, and one a brigantine, which stood in for the land, there were two French ships, one of 30 guns. I had before been informed that the three Admirals which had always worn flags til now had all the money, therefore I thought if we could get these 3, it would be the best service; accordingly I called to the Kingston, *which was near me, to attack the Vice Admiral, and sent my boat to the* Portland *to engage the Rear Admiral, and I made sail up to the Admiral and engaged him. I thought I had no need to make use of the Fire ship so kept to windward before night thinking the* Kingston *nor* Portland *not to comply as expected with my directions, I made a signal for a line of battle . . . It was just sunset when I began to engage the Admiral, and in about an hour and a half it being then quite dark the Admiral blew up I being then along his side, not half pistols shot from him, so that the heat of the blast came very hot upon us, and several splinters of plank and timber came on board us afire, but we soon threw them overboard. I presumed the ship did not blow all up into the air, because there was little or no blow, but I believe the ships sides blew out, for she caused a sea that came in at our ports, she immediately sunk with all her riches, which must have been very great.*

All her riches were great indeed—the greatest treasure as yet unfound lying at the bottom of the sea.

The Spanish declarations described events leading up to the engagement and battle. Captain Don Joseph Canis de Alzamora was in command of the *Urca de Nietto.* The *Nietto* was well-armed with, "22 iron cannons of 18 pound ball in the lower deck, and about 8 cannon of 3 pound ball on the upper deck," according to Captain Alzamora.

Reading the captain of the *Nietto's* declaration, it is clear that he placed blame for the disaster on Admiral Villanueva's lack of preparation and carelessness.

"I came on board the *Urca de Nietto* with 48 soldiers and sailors, including my staff. The *Urca* had on board 30 sailors, 34 ordinary seamen, a few page boys and its officers. Of this number, 20 of them were infirm. Although the Captain General [Villanueva] was petitioned for more artillery men, none were given," Captain Alzamora said.

Of the departure from Porto Bello and the battle off Cartagena, the commander of the *Nietto* declared:

At 9 a.m., from aloft, 4 ship's sails were seen to the north. The wind was coming from the ENE and the galleons were coasting along the islands in search of port. Lacking a NNW wind the said enemy warships were going to fall in with the galleons . . . at 4:30 p.m. the Capitana changed course to seaward with the

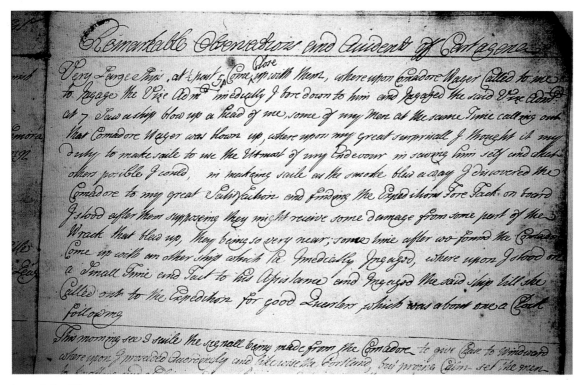

Log of the *Kingston*.

Almiranta to his east and the Urca de Nietto *downwind of both the Capitana and Almiranta. After some confusion the battle line was formed as follows: Gobierno, French ship* Santo Spiritis, *the* Urca de Nietto, *and the Capitana. It was now 5 p.m. and the English started fighting with the Almiranta who promptly replied with his broadsides, and the fight continued with the English Commander coming for the Capitana.*

It being a clear shot to the Urca [de Nietto] *enroute the English Commander gave his broadside to the* Urca *and the* Urca *responded with a few cannon. The fight continued until the English Commander and the Capitana were in the same place at nightfall.*

The exchange of cannon fire was brutal. Captain Alzamora described it tersely. "The *Urca* was responding with all the firepower it could muster, and for this the *Urca* and the Capitana were both receiving damaging blows. One broadside of 24 cannon disabled a gun on the *Urca's* lower deck, damaged a launch, and the Forecastle stanchion and ladder . . ."

The *Urca de Nietto* ran for safety. Unable to escape, Captain Alzamora ran his ship aground

The author after surfacing with Spanish treasure.

and blew it up. The log of the HMS *Kingston* recites the event:

June 1 [of the English Julian calendar] . . . About 3 this afternoon we see a large ship come out of the Grand Barue, which I suppose was the said galleon, that lay there at anchor. Before in a very little time afterwards he bore away for the Brue again, we being still in chase of him about 6 O'clock in the evening he run ashore upon the west end of ye Barue with all his sailes . . . and the same time set her on fire, at 7 O'clock we got in and anchored about a mile distant from

the galleone, at which time I suppose the fire got in to his powder room, and blew her up.

TREASURE AWAITS

There it was. The *Urca de Nietto* grounded, set afire, and blown up on an island. The *San Jose* blown apart at sea. The prize ship Gobierno captured. The Almiranta laden with a treasure equal to that aboard *San Jose* was pursued by the *Kingston* and *Portland*. The English ships gave off the chase when they reached the shoals near Boca Chica passage into Cartagena harbor. Thus the Spanish ship escaped, as did

Chinese K'ang shi rice bowl recovered from the galleon *Maravillas*.

the rest of the Spanish fleet that sailed along the coast and safely made it into the harbor.

"They towed the Gobierno into Jamaica pretty well torn up. So ended the battle. The other ships hugged the coast and got into Cartagena that way. As the English were approaching her, the *Nietto* exploded. I know where she blew up," Bob Weller said.

"The *Urca de Nietto* blew up on an island where my lawyer in Bogotá had his summer house. He was going to let us use that house for the expedition," Weller added.

Political turmoil in Colombia, assassinations, insurgencies, rebellions, out-of-control drug lords, and drug trafficking made the situation untenable for the Wellers and their team of explorers to continue the search for the remains of the *San Jose*.

The Spanish galleon still remains on the bottom, the richest treasure yet unfound.

Utensils had to be brought aboard ship by officers and crew members. These are examples of spoons and forks and a knife recovered from sunken Spanish vessels.

THE 1715 FLEET

t was an ill wind that stormed across the Atlantic Ocean on July 29, 1715. For Philip V of Spain, the hurricane would sink his entire treasure fleet bound up the coast of Florida from Cuba with gold and silver, specie and bullion, the output of Spanish colonial mints in the New World for the last four years.

Gold chain. Each link weighs one ounce. Passengers and merchants wore heavy gold jewelry to evade the 20 percent tax to the Crown.

PRELUDE TO TRAGEDY

Most of the ships were thrown up and wrecked on shallow reefs and shoals near the beach. Some supposedly sank in deep water with all hands and have not been found. So furious was the hurricane that 700 passengers and crew lost their lives within sight of land. Only a small privateer—a French ship that joined the con- voy for protection—escaped destruction, testi- mony to the caprice of nature's fury.

While tales about the sinking, efforts to salvage the treasure by the Spanish themselves, attacks and looting of the salvage camp, and modern discovery of the sunken treasure are many, no story is better told than the tale of veteran diver Bob Weller.

The pottery shard with Bob Weller's writing, describing his find of the fabulous 11'2" gold chain.

THE GOLD CHAIN

"This shard was recovered 3' from an 11'-2" gold chain by 'FROGFOOT' BOB WELLER ON JUNE 22, 1991 'NIEVES', Weller wrote on a ten-by-four-inch, irregularly shaped, ocher-colored chunk of a Spanish pottery jar. The shard sits on a shelf in Weller's office in his home in Lake Worth, Florida. It is propped up on a little stand, evidence of a day that will forever stand out in the annals of treasure hunting: the day of the gold chain.

Perhaps it was not the most valuable, not the most beautiful, not the most unusual artifact found amidst the wreckage of the 1715 treasure fleet, but for Bob "Frogfoot" Weller, his wife Margaret, and diver Bob Luyendyk, it was a glorious find. The gold chain measured eleven feet, two inches and was about 22.3 carats of pure soft yellow gold.

"It was Sunday, June 22, 1991," Weller began to tell the tale, the wedge-shaped chunk of pottery with the legend of his find scrawled upon it in his hand. Weller's reminiscence halted as he turned the chunk of pottery over and examined it, as if the memory might have been a wonderful dream he could relive only by being in contact with the reality of the object in his hands, as if this chunk of fired clay earthenware was a touchstone that made the story real.

"A flat calm day. Absolutely great viz that day when we came out Fort Pierce inlet. There was just Bob Luyendyk, Margaret, and me on *Pandion*," Weller said. *Pandion* was the Wellers' salvage boat, a small, wide-beamed converted fish trap boat built in Perrine, Florida, and a lucky boat for the Wellers. Its shallow draft let them navigate in between the reefs where treasure had gotten wedged when the 1715 fleet was broken up by ocean storms.

Weller was up in the bow. "'Man it's going to be a good day,' I thought. I could see the bottom," Weller recounted, turning the pottery shard in his hands.

"We headed out to Jewelry Flat. That's what the salvors named it. Every hole had gold jewelry in what we called *monkey holes*. This time when we got out to Jewelry Flat, John Brandon was anchored over it with 300 feet of anchor rope. John was on my site. He had taken it over. I started to say I'd work elsewhere, but then I said, 'I want to work the site.' I dropped my bow anchor over his stern anchor. I gave John an A-OK signal. He gave me back an A-OK. I'd known John for a long time. We positioned *Pandion* within four feet of the edge of the reef," Frogfoot recounted.

"Bob Luyendyk went in the water first. He was always first. Didn't find anything in the first hole," Weller said.

Pandion had a mailbox that could be lowered over its propeller. The contraption was in an elbow shape. With the treasure salvage vessel securely anchored at the bow and stern, anchors out to each side, the ship was held in place. It could be moved and repositioned on the anchor lines. With the mailbox secured over the propeller and the engine engaged, the downward stream of water would blow a hole in the sand right under the boat.

Divers would work in the hole as the sand was blown away. With proper speed, the prop deflector would not blow too fast, and treasure could be recovered from where it settled on the hard coral substrate under layers of ocean sand.

"About eleven o'clock Margaret and I went in and worked the bottom until one thirty. Got up, had lunch, and Bob went back down. He came up about three thirty. He didn't find a thing. At three thirty I went down by myself. Margaret stayed up on the boat," Weller said.

A LUCKY WIND

"The wind picked up to fifteen knots out of the east. We were being pushed toward the beach. At 4 p.m., John Brandon decided he'd pick up anchors and go home. John sent Mike McGuire in a small boat to pick up his stern anchor. Our tag line was wrapped around their anchor line," Weller related.

"He couldn't get their anchor up. Brandon was hollering, 'We got to go.' Mike got a face mask from the boat, came back up and said it's tangled. Margaret and Luyendyk let loose our bowline. *Pandion* pushed back seventy-five feet. Mike got the tag line untangled and said, 'I'm free,' and pulled their anchor," Weller smiled, remembering his predicament underwater.

"I'm on the bottom being pulled along. I go along for the ride," he explained. Divers were supplied by regulator hoses that drew air from a compressor on board the *Pandion*.

"Finally *Pandion* stabilized. Bob and Margaret could not pull *Pandion* back against the wind to where it had been anchored. They gave me two tugs on the air hose to see if I wanted to blow a hole. I signaled up from the bottom 'yes.'"

"The first hole had this pottery shard," Weller smiled. "I had a metal detector so stuck the shard under my arm. They gave me two tugs. I said 'Yes, blow a hole.' They did. I saw the chain. I knew what it was. I checked with the metal detector to see if there was any more and came up," he said.

"Bob Luyendyk and I were at the wheel. All we heard were bubbles," Margaret said.

Weller related what happened next, "I had the metal detector. I couldn't let go of the stern of the boat or I'd go down. I had my weight belt on, had to keep the regulator in my mouth. Finally they came back to the stern. I handed Margaret the gold chain," Weller said. One can imagine him wearing heavy diving weights, both hands full, unable to remove his regulator, grunting through its mouthpiece.

"It measured eleven feet, two inches," Margaret said.

By the time the Wellers returned the next day, diver Duke Long had found a low-carat gold ring on the site they had worked. "We'd of been better not to have marked the spot," Margaret laughed. She described the friendly and sometimes not so friendly competition to find treasure from the wreckage of Spain's 1715 fleet.

EARLY HISTORY OF THE TREASURE COAST AND SPANISH FLEETS

In the days of Spanish conquest, the Atlantic coast of Florida was wild. Indians inhabited the higher ground and frequented beaches to fish and gather shellfish. Today it is called the

Bob Weller in front of the shipwreck painting with the gold chain he found.

Treasure Coast, a thin strip of land between the Atlantic Ocean on the east and the navigable Intracoastal Waterway on the west.

The 1715 fleet wrecked and was tossed helter skelter by the force of the hurricane from an area south of present-day Fort Pierce to about Sebastian Inlet, south of Melbourne, Florida.

Treasure fleets gathered in Havana. Ships that voyaged from Spain to Veracruz on the Gulf Coast of Mexico were called the Nueva España Flota. Ships that made landfall farther south at ports in Colombia and Panama were called the Tierra Firme Flota.

Spain had Manila galleons that plied the Pacific Ocean, making port at the crown's established colonies in the Philippines. Trade with China and Japan had started. Coveted Chinese porcelain and Japanese silks were shipped in these Manila galleons to Acapulco on Mexico's Pacific coast.

These cargoes were then carried on the backs of mules and slaves overland to Veracruz. The delicate cargoes of porcelains and Chinese and Japanese fabrics, spices, and trade goods were then transshipped aboard galleons heading back to Spain.

Trade fairs sprung up along the coast at Veracruz in mosquito-infested shantytowns. Merchants and captains who owned the vessels sold their manufactured goods imported from Europe for gold and silver coins to merchants who journeyed to the fair with trade goods from the colonies.

The crown's output from New World mints, gold and silver coins, and bullion from silver mines in Mexico and Potosi in the then-viceroyalty of Peru were loaded on heavily armed galleons of the king.

Sailing from Veracruz, the first port of call was made at Havana, Cuba. Cuba was Spain's convoying up point. Ships from the various fleets would rendezvous in Havana Harbor. Merchants would load more cargo of trade goods such as hides, dyes, fruit, and tobacco and take on fresh water and supplies for the trip back to Spain.

If repairs still had to be made to the vessels, this was the last chance before heading into the Straits of Florida between Cuba and the Florida coast, up along the Keys and then the mainland using the Gulf Stream's northward-flowing current to push the sailing ships homeward across the Ocean Sea.

THE FLEET OF 1715

The 1715 treasure fleet was made up of Captain-General Don Juan Esteban de Ubilla's Nueva España Fleet's five ships, and joined by General Antonio Echeverz y Zubiza's six Tierra Firma Fleet vessels in Havana. Captain Antoine d'Aire of the French ship *Grifon* received permission to join the treasure fleet for protection. D'Aire left Havana with the convoy and its 14 million pesos in gold and silver.

The voyage of the fleet that would end in disaster began in Spain where General Ubilla set out aboard the Capitana of the Nueva España Fleet, a ship named *Nuestra Señora de la Regala*, a 471-ton vessel. It carried fifty cannons for defense against pirates and enemy ships.

General Ubilla discovered once at sea that there were 134 people who had stowed away aboard the small ship, which meant there would be a shortage of food and water. It took fifty days to reach landfall on Puerto Rico before they could replenish supplies of fresh water, by now a precious commodity.

Ubilla had begun the voyage with eight ships in his fleet. Then a hurricane struck in September 1714, and Ubilla lost one ship of his flota. On March 8, 1715, another hurricane hit Veracruz. Ubilla lost three more ships. It was a prelude to the final disaster Ubilla would face on his return to Spain.

General Ubilla finally made it across the Gulf of Mexico to Veracruz. On March 28, 1715, as if a portent to what fate would later await General Ubilla, a storm blew the *Nuestra Señora de la Regala* onto a reef.

To save the *Regala*, her masts had to be chopped away. Repairs were tediously made by shipwrights in Veracruz. The vessel was eventually loaded with treasure, which appeared on her manifest, and contraband smuggled aboard to evade the Spanish Royal Fifth tax. Passengers came aboard with their personal treasures in jewelry.

A king's ransom was stowed in the overloaded holds of the *Regala*. There were more than 1,300 chests of coins that the Spanish counted to the coin, worth 2,559,917 pesos. There were chests of silver ornaments, gold bars, cochineal (a brilliantly colored, vivid red dye squeezed from bugs), indigo, chocolate and

vanilla beans, copper, tanned hides, four chests of Chinese porcelain wares, wood, pottery jars, and balsam.

Ubilla loaded the cargo, the output of the mint in Mexico City and the goods brought overland from the Pacific trade, aboard his remaining ships and sailed for Havana on May 1, 1715. He arrived with four ships on June 24, 1715. Ubilla's fleet consisted of his Capitana, the *Nuestra Señora de la Regala*, the Almiranta, *Santo Cristo de San Roman*, a smaller refuerzo named the *Urca de Lima*, and a patache *Nuestra Señora de las Nieves*. The convoy was joined by Ubilla's frigatilla, a small boat made in Cuba.

The two fleets—Ubilla's Nueva España and Echeverz's Tierra Firme—would join together for the trip back to Spain in Havana.

Don Echeverz and his Tierra Firme Fleet had made a lucky voyage from Spain to the New World. He was troubled by inconvenience but prizes he captured more than made up for delays he suffered when the treasure he was to pick up in Cartagena had been transported instead from Peru to Porto Bello. From his first landfall near Puerto Rico, Echeverz dispatched his vessel *San Miguel* to Havana to load tobacco. The three other ships under his command proceeded to Cartagena, then to Porto Bello in Panama.

When their cargoes of trade goods from Spain were unloaded, Echeverz sent his three ships out to pick up enemy prizes or smugglers. His captains did well. They captured three ships. One was the Dutch galley or frigate *Holandesa* taken off Punta Bernardo, fifty miles west of Cartagena. Prizes officially belonged to the crown, but the captors could claim salvage.

With his award, Don Echeverz bought the *Holandesa* at the public auction held in Porto Bello. Archive records indicate that Don Echeverz paid 2,000 pesos for the ship and renamed it for his patron saint *Nuestra Señora del Carmen*. Contemporary salvors recalled the Dutch captain's name noted as *Señor de la Popa* by the Spanish, and use it to prevent confusion with Echeverz's larger vessel.

Echeverz's squadron captured a French ship near Porto Bello. Archive documents record he was also able to buy this ship at auction for 4,125 pesos. Echeverz also named this ship *Nuestra Señora del Carmen*. With so many ships of the same name, the French vessel was commonly called *El Ciervo*, meaning the stag.

Still marauding for prizes, Echeverz's ships captured a small vessel named *San Miguel de Excelsis*. Echeverz put a crew of fifteen officers and men aboard and sent it to Havana.

Echeverz arrived in Havana on October 2, 1714. The little English prize renamed *San Miguel de Excelsis* was there and now joined by Echeverz's squadron consisting of the Capitana, *Nuestra Señora del Carmen*; the Almiranta, *Nuestra Señora del Rosario*; the naos *Concepcion* and *San Miguel*; the Dutch prize *Holandesa* (*Señor de la Popa*, so as not to be confused with the others); and the French prize *El Ciervo*.

Echeverz's ships carried trade goods for the colonies from Spain. He also carried 150 soldiers, papers, and mercury to refine precious metals like silver and gold. The *Rosario* off-loaded her cargo and picked up 15,514 pesos of gold. The manifest listed silver, hides, cacao, wood, and gifts loaded aboard the 312-ton *Rosario*.

Delay after delay held the combined fleet of eleven Spanish ships and the French vessel *Grifon* in Havana Harbor until July 27, 1715. This was well into hurricane season.

The trip back to Spain would follow time-honored navigation patterns from Havana. The vessels would head across and through the Strait of Florida and up the coast of the mainland—keeping in the northward-flowing Gulf Stream in sight of land, where landmarks and soundings were recorded in the sailing directions. At a latitude of about where Cape Hatteras is today, they would head out across the open Atlantic.

One thing the Spanish had learned after the wrecking of many of their ships upon the shoals and reefs of Florida waters was that they had to leave Havana before the season when the great winds came.

Ships making back to Spain from Cuba sailed between the Bahama Islands and the Florida coast. This narrow channel gave them about fifty miles to get through a neck of ocean. It was wide enough to sail seaward, but Spanish navigators preferred to determine their position by landfall and prominent coastal features.

General Ubilla knew bad weather was coming. Hurricanes blew from the northeast in the summer, from the southwest in the winter. Gale- and hurricane-force winds could swirl around and change direction once they hit the Florida mainland. It was summer. The captain-general of the fleet of twelve heavily laden treasure ships knew his fleet was in jeopardy when he reached the Bahama Channel.

HURRICANE IN THE ATLANTIC

Ubilla's fleet was only out of Havana a couple of days when hurricane winds struck. The ships were somewhere off the coast of Florida, but navigation was impossible in the fury of sea and wind. The ships in the flota were owned by merchants and captains under contract and licensed by the crown. Private contractors of the day took the risks of the voyage, fitted out their ships, and traded in the New World so long as the taxes were paid. The royal cargoes of the output of the mints of Mexico and Peru were transported on armed Spanish military ships, for the most part.

The commanders did everything to save their ships and valuable cargoes. *Nuestra Señora del Carmen* battened down hatches and reefed sails in the fury of the wind. Waves crashed over the bow from the east. The *Carmen's* bowsprit was torn away. The ship's masts crashed down and waves broke through stern windows smashed by their fury.

The *Carmen* was still afloat. It was pushed like a frail waif across the ocean toward the coast of Florida. It is not likely that Echeverz could see the shoreline, but when he heard the surf breaking, he ordered bow anchors thrown over.

The *Carmen* swung on her anchor cable while Echeverz ordered the vessel lightened. Cannons were thrown over, it was reported, but nothing saved the ship. It was dragged

McLarty Treasure Museum, which is built on the campsite of the Spanish salvors.

under at the bows by the fury of the waves as the cables holding her against them by anchors caught in shallow water.

The *Carmen* struck a reef not a thousand feet from shore in water about twenty feet deep. It rolled and sank. The passengers and crew of the *Carmen* fared better than most of the hurricane's victims, and many gained the relative safety of the beach.

None of the ships in the convoy escaped, except the *Grifon*, the French privateer commanded by Captain d'Aire who outdistanced the fleet, sailing away northward.

UBILLA'S FATE

Waves, driven by the fury of hurricane winds, washed over Ubilla's ship. By the early morning hours of July 29, 1715, sailors and passengers cowered, prayed, and gave each other confession. Seamen were hurled overboard trying to reef and reduce sail.

General Ubilla and his son were lost when the *Regala* was thrown up on the reef, on what is today Wabasso Beach south of Sebastian Inlet. The *Regala* was heaved upon the shore with such force that her decks were sheared apart.

The *Regala's* lower deck was wedged on a reef about 300 yards from shore, the upper decks broken apart and strewn about on the inshore reefs and rocks; timbers and rigging were thrown upon the wild sandy beach—even up into the tangled growth beyond the beach itself.

When the winds subsided the admiral in command, Don Francisco Salmon, had survived. His ship, designated the Almiranta, the *Santo Cristo de San Roman*, was wrecked.

The admiral organized a search for survivors. Bodies were pulled from the surf. When an accounting was made, over 700 passengers and crew perished in the storm. Treasure was everywhere—in the hulls of the wrecked ships, strewn upon the beaches, dunes, and mangroves.

When the winds died away, mosquitos and bugs attacked the survivors. Admiral Salmon formed camps to tend to them. He sent runners north to the Spanish fort at St. Augustine for help and began to pile treasure up on the beach. The survivors made shelters from flotsam that washed ashore.

THE *San Roman*

Admiral Salmon's ship, the *San Roman*, was almost as full of treasure as Captain-General Ubilla's *Regala*. The *San Roman* displaced 450 tons and carried fifty-four cannons aboard. It was the largest of the fleet. The Almiranta in a treasure fleet brought up the rear of the convoy to offer protection, thus the need for heavy armament.

Spanish archives that detail the *San Roman's* cargo revealed that 611,412 pesos of gold were taken by the king as his Royal Fifth tax. The *San Roman* carried 684 chests of gold and silver coins valued at 2,687,416 pesos. Like the cargo aboard General Ubilla's ship, the *San Roman* had sacks, chests, and bags of cochineal, indigo, leather hides, gifts, earthenware jugs, copper sheets, fourteen chests of Chinese porcelain wares, sarsaparilla, and brazilwood.

It became impossible for *San Roman's* Captain Juan de Equilaz to control his ship once the fury of the hurricane struck. They lost sight of the rest of the fleet and struggled to keep their own ship afloat after the masts and rudder were torn away.

The *San Roman* struck a shallow reef about six miles south of the *Regala*, north of present-day Vero Beach. The ship hit bottom about a quarter mile offshore, was thrown shoreward, and kept hitting bottom as the waves crashed over the helpless wooden craft.

Salvors discovered a scattering of cannons and ballast stones along the path the *San Roman* took heading to her final resting place. The ship grounded and was smashed by the fury of the ocean in twelve feet of water, within a cable's length of shore. Water filled the hull. The wind and waves worked the shipwreck apart until the bow was torn off, its stern torn away, and the gun deck smashed. Cannons were scattered over the reef, attesting to the power of the storm.

THE *Carmen*

South of the *San Roman* just off Vero Beach lies the wreckage of *Nuestra Señora del Carmen*.

The *Carmen's* gun deck was 150 feet, 6 inches, the keel about 25 feet shorter. The vessel displaced 1,072 tons. It was a massive ship for her time, originally fitted out by the English to carry seventy-two cannons. In 1713, prior to her voyage to the New World, many cannons were removed to make room for cargo.

THE *Rosario*

Posted to bring up the rear of the convoy, the *Rosario* acted as a shepherd with her forty guns, in the event of attack on the fleet. The *Rosario* sailed within sight of what is now Tavernier in the Florida Keys. Ship design had changed since the ungainly naos Columbus sailed across the Ocean Sea. Many older vessels still lumbered along at about four to seven knots. But faster sailing ships with sleek hulls, which had better water displacement qualities, routinely made the Atlantic crossing more quickly.

From the vicinity of Tavernier, when the hurricane winds first struck, the *Rosario* was blown far north and crashed on the reefs south of Vero Beach, at a place now offshore of the Rio Mar Golf Course at Sandy Point. Echeverz's son was killed along with 123 passengers and crew. The *Rosario's* cannons and ballast were scattered over the inshore area.

Urca de Lima

South of the site where the *Rosario* struck, Ubilla's refuerzo—the *Santisima Trinidad y Nuestra Señora de la Concepcion*, captained by Miguel de Lima—came ashore. Ships of the day had to be inscribed by clerks and sailors. The shorthand notation used for the *Concepcion* was *Urca*, meaning ship, and the captain's last name, Miguel de Lima y Melo. Thus the vessel was known as the *Urca de Lima*. It displaced 350 tons, was built in Holland, and shipped twenty cannons.

Miguel de Lima y Melo described the events:

> *The sun disappeared and the wind increased in velocity coming from the east and east northeast. The seas became very giant in size, the wind continued blowing us toward shore, pushing us into shallow water. It soon happened that we were unable to use any sail at all, making bare our yards, mostly due to the wind carrying away our sails and rigging, and we were at the mercy of the wind and water, always driven closer to shore. Having then lost all of our masts, all of the ships were wrecked on the shore, and with the exception of mine, broke to pieces. We lost only thirty seamen and marines, who were carried away by waves while in the waist of the ship. My ship is at Palmar de Ays in 27 degrees and 15 minutes at the mouth of a river.*

The *Urca de Lima* carried the king's lawyer and principal representative aboard, Alonso de Armenta de la Vega. De la Vega survived and was the man put in charge of supervising salvage efforts on site to recover as much treasure from the sunken fleet as possible.

By dropping his anchor between the two parallel reefs that run north and south along the coast, Captain de Lima managed to save his ship. The anchor held, although a mast broke and became tangled by rigging around the ship's hull. The *Urca de Lima* sank when shifting winds brought the vessel down on the anchor's fluke, holing the hull.

When the storm passed over, *Urca de Lima* sat upright on the bottom with superstructure and cabins above the surface. The ship's two launches were saved and repaired, and Captain de Lima's ship was made the headquarters.

Captain de Lima wrote:

On these deserted beaches, which were very barren and dry, God permitted us to find sweet water, enough to drink, by making wells the height of a man, which were called casimbas. *However, all of the survivors were not able to survive the temperament of those shores, the heat of the sun was insufferable, and the number of mosquitos were probably greater than the plague. Thanks to God all of the silver on my ship has escaped.*

Author with Bob Weller in front of artifacts from Weller's finds.

Supplies were taken from the ship's stores and given to victims who survived the storm. Survivors gathered on the beach.

The *Urca de Lima* was laden with hides, chocolate, spices like vanilla and sassafras, and private treasure in chests and sacks. Treasure was recovered from the *Urca de Lima's* holds and stacked up on her deck, which was above water. Captain de Lima ordered his launches to get help, one northward to St. Augustine, the other back to Havana. The captain and his crew remained aboard the vessel for a month, faring better than those unfortunate survivors on the beaches who sought relief from ravenous hordes of mosquitos by burying themselves in sand.

The *Urca de Lima's* manifest registered 252,171 pesos of silver, silver ornaments, 132 chests that were denominated "gifts" that likely contained uncut emeralds. There were thirty-two chests of Chinese porcelain, as well as the general cargo.

Supplies arrived from Havana to support the victims of the hurricane and salvors thirty-one days after the wrecking. While the *Urca de Lima's* cargo was salvaged, the Spanish decided to burn the ship to the waterline to conceal it from English freebooters. The *Urca de Lima* was eventually covered by sand, its timbers below the waterline eaten by teredo worms and the shipwreck forgotten.

When modern-day salvors discovered the remains of the *Urca de Lima*—opposite Fort Pierce's old inlet and one mile north of the present inlet at Fort Pierce—the ballast rocks were intact.

The river rocks formed a neat heap eight-feet high. The mound was about seventy by twenty feet between the reefs. Silver bullion shaped like wedges of cheese were recovered from the site, along with large lumps of conglomerate. Uncut emeralds and many gold coins were brought up by divers on the site, located just off the beach very close to shore. Early salvors called it the *Wedge Wreck* because of the silver wedges recovered.

Fort Pierce officials used some of the cannons recovered from the *Urca de Lima* site to grace the outside of City Hall. The state of Florida granted the last salvage permits for the *Urca de Lima* in 1984. The next year, the hull was mapped by underwater archaeologists, and plans were made to create an underwater park on the site. In 1987, the *Urca de Lima* became Florida's first Underwater Archaeological Preserve and was listed on the National Register of Historic Places in 2001. A plaque marks the location underwater. The wreck site is located at the north end of Pepper Park on Highway A1A in about ten to fifteen feet of water some two hundred yards off the beach. Divers are welcome to visit and dive on the site, but the site cannot be disturbed nor can artifacts be removed.

THE *Nieves*

In the days of segregation, Florida had beaches reserved for blacks. The beach is now called Frederick Douglas Park; but in the 1950s and 1960s, at the time salvors began finding coins from the wrecked 1715 fleet on its shores, it was called Colored Beach. It was here that Captain-General Ubilla's small patache, the *Nuestra Señora de las Nieves y las Animas*, wrecked. The little ship was only 192.5 tons and carried a dozen cannons. Built in Portugal, the *Nieves's* design followed classical lines with three decks and a high quarterdeck.

The *Nieves* was captained by Francisco de Soto Sanchez. Sanchez owned the vessel with a Dutchman who acted as ship's master, Esteban Pieters. The *Nieves's* manifest registered 44,000 pesos in gold aboard. The shipwreck was not worked by Spanish salvors of the day,

A gold shipwreck coin showing the Hapsburg shield with all of the nations belonging to the dynasty.

A gold shipwreck coin showing a Crusader's cross.

A gold coin, beautifully stamped, showing the Pillars of Hercules and the Spanish legend PLUS ULTRA: "There is more beyond."

who concentrated their efforts on the larger vessels over the next four years after the fleet wrecked.

Since the *Nieves* was privately co-owned by its captain and master, unregistered smuggled treasure was concealed in the ship's hull. Modern-day salvage divers recovered gold and silver bars without royal tax stamps, indicating they were contraband.

Emerald studded rings and gold jewelry were recovered from the *Nieves* site. One of the most fabulous treasure finds ever recovered from the 1715 treasure fleet was discovered by Bob Weller and his team on the *Nieves* site in 1985.

Weller brought up a golden rosary with a six-foot chain. The rosary is separated by delicate gold filigree work with precious stones and pearls. Divers located gold rings studded with

emeralds. One large ring that was recovered contained a rectangular-cut, 10.5-carat emerald.

A finely crafted golden reliquary, an ornate container that may have held a lock of hair of a loved one, was recovered from the *Nieves* site in 1987. The twelve feet of chain made of delicate filigree assayed at 22 carats and ended in a magnificent brooch. Gold coins, emerald-studded earrings, pendants, a gold snuffbox, an ornate golden prayer book cover, and Royal Escudo coins made the *Nieves* a legendary treasure wreck for modern-day salvage divers like the Wellers.

Bob Weller and Whitey Keevan—so named for the color of his hair—recorded the find of the rosary in the log of the *Defiance*, their 31-foot Bertram salvage vessel as it left Fort Pierce Inlet at 9 a.m. on July 14, 1985. Weller's log records: "9:20 – Arrived *Nieves* site. Seas unusually calm with winds SE at 5 kts. Water clear with visibility 20' or more."

A few minutes later a diver went overside, and the blower over the propeller was engaged to remove sand from the site. Weller recorded in the log: "9:45 – Whitey over the side, and engines blowing at 600 rpm. Sandy flat bottom with depth of sand 6-8' over Anastasia [limestone] rock."

Weller and Keevan were diving on a site that Mel Fisher had picked over. Mel left to head south when pickings got slim and it looked like Fisher's research had finally located where the *Atocha* had gone down off Key West. Subcontractors like Weller and Keevan were left to work for shares of what they would find on the 1715 fleet.

An artist, Larissa Dillin, rendering a gold chain and cross found on the 1715 fleet.

The weather off Fort Pierce, where they were working about three miles south of the inlet, was difficult to predict. Two reef lines ran parallel to shore; one, a mostly sanded-over rocky ridge just off the beach; the second, a little more than a cable length out. It was between these reefs that a lot of treasure spilled. Outside the reef line, treasure settled down through the sand and was on the limestone bedrock. A thick layer of sand had to be blown away to get at it.

Working in shallow water, often only eight to ten feet deep, with the mailbox overhead, sea conditions had to be almost perfect to keep the salvage vessel from being thrown up and down in the waves, thus bringing the heavy mailbox down on the diver working below. The Fort Pierce Inlet created a lot of dirty water along the coast, limiting visibility that was made worse when the ocean was churned up by wind.

For Bob and Whitey July 14, 1985, was a perfect day. Whitey worked underwater for more than an hour, then came up to rest. Bob Weller went overside with his metal detector. When a stern anchor aboard the salvage vessel slipped, *Defiance* swung away from Weller who had to follow the pull since he was breathing from an air hose supplied by a compressor on board the ship. With the propeller

One of the gold chains found by Bob Weller.

still engaged, *Defiance* was still digging, blowing sand out of a hole.

Weller was moving to where the mailbox was digging. His metal detector buzzed. It was a lead bullet. Weller kept swimming underwater toward the hole being dug. In the morning's unusually good visibility, he could see about fifty feet underwater. The metal detector buzzed again as he worked it back and forth over the sandy bottom, making his way to the new hole the blower was digging.

"I got another hit. I expected another .22 slug as I fanned down through 6–8 inches of sand," Weller wrote in his classic book about the 1715 fleet, *Sunken Treasure on Florida Reefs*.

What Weller fanned away was filigree gold, finely worked and separated from the rest of the medallion by ebony beads. It was a golden cross. When the initial excitement waned and other divers were called to come over, the filigree cross was passed to another boat to be taken back to Fort Pierce. Keevan decided to go back underwater and try his luck.

When he surfaced again, he handed Weller a sixty-inch golden necklace. The delicately worked filigree was separated by the same ebony beads as the cross and medallions. The discovery would complete the rosary and became the single most important artifact discovered on the 1715 fleet—that is until Bob and

Margaret Weller and their team of divers found the Queen's Jewels.

Everything was meticulously recorded on ships' manifests by scribes working for Spain's House of Trade. The Casa de Contratación governed all commerce to and from the colonies in the New World. It was a monopoly. The crown took a Royal Fifth, 20 percent of all goods convoyed back to Spain. The crown licensed merchants and captains to trade with the colonies.

Since jewelry bought from Spain was not taxed, merchants and passengers often lied about the origins of their jewelry, using a loophole in the laws. They carried thick, pure gold ornaments back to Spain, while their personal treasure chests bulged with ornately worked gold often studded with emeralds from mines in Colombia and cut by craftsmen and jewelry makers in Mexico.

Bob and Margaret Weller received a subcontract to work a wreck site that was located off the beach, about two miles south of Sebastian Inlet, directly in front of the cabin of treasure hunter legend Kip Wagner.

Kip Wagner was a Florida beachcomber who began discovering gold and silver coins washed up on the beaches from Fort Pierce to Sebastian after every storm. He organized a treasure salvage operation in the early days and found the ocean bottom paved with gold coins. Kip built a house right on the beach where he could look out and see his shipwreck sites.

Kip was long dead on July 1, 1993, but his cabin still remained where the legendary treasure diver had built it. The cabin was a land-mark for divers working the *Nuestra Señora de la Regala*, Captain-General Ubilla's Capitana.

The Wellers knew the area had been worked by Kip Wagner and his divers as well as teams of other salvagers over time. What is evident for anyone who has worked a treasure site in the ocean is that there is always something that has been overlooked. Patience invariably pays dividends.

The Wellers brought their twenty-five-foot salvage boat *Pandion* in between the reefs. In this area, the near reef was 175 feet from shore. The little salvage vessel was anchored and set to work over an area that Bob Weller selected. They took their bearings from markers on shore, made log entries, and the team began diving in relays.

Using a Garrett pulse induction metal detector, one member of the team put on a scuba tank and decided to check around rocks farther away from the boat.

Bob Weller had been a commander in the U.S. Navy in World War II. He became the commanding officer of Underwater Demolition Team One during his service in Korea. He was used to command under wartime conditions. An easygoing, disciplined man, Weller would make suggestions, but salvage operations were free and easy aboard *Pandion*. There was plenty of room for taking a chance, following a clue or instinct that something might be found slightly off the site being worked.

The rest of the team went underwater with the hookah rig, surface-supplied regulators that fed off a gasoline-powered compressor

The gold brooch with blue and white diamonds found by the Weller team on the 1715 fleet.

Earrings found by the Weller team just off the beach from the 1715 fleet. First only one earring was discovered. The team later found the matching earring.

aboard the *Pandion*. When the team member swam back to the ship and handed up a gold brooch studded with diamonds, there was pandemonium aboard *Pandion*.

These were the Queen's Jewels—if not officially, by Spanish archival records, then they should have been. It was a story from the annals of piracy on the Spanish Main where chests of gold brimmed over with a fortune in booty.

The Weller team wasted no time in getting an organized search pattern underway to see what else could be found where the team member found the gold brooch.

The team systematically searched the area where the first find was made. A *lazo* (a round pendant) was found, as well as a gold drop earring. The brooch was studded with 177 blue white diamonds. The top part, the lazo, contained 127 diamonds. The gold earring had fifty-four diamonds in it. The team quit the site reluctantly, determined to return with the next morning's dawn.

Bob Luyendyk joined the Weller team that morning. He had been diving weekends with them and now took off from work to join the hunt for more jewelry.

Luyendyk surfaced around noon. He found a golden dragon that the Spanish used to pick their ears and teeth, the second section of the gold lazo that contained seventeen diamonds, gold rings, and the matching earring to the pair.

These two days in July 1993 will forever be remembered in the annals of maritime salvage. The golden filigree rosary was found in 1985. Bob Weller's eleven-foot, two-inch gold chain came up in 1991. The year of the Queen's Jewels was 1993. The husband and wife team of Bob and Margaret Weller became the Deans of Underwater Treasure Divers. Their ship *Pandion*, the converted twenty-five-foot trap boat, entered the annals of maritime history as having recovered more than $5 million in treasure.

The wrecks so far salvaged off the coast of Fort Pierce are just six of the ships that

Map made by Bob Weller to mark areas searched south of Sebastian Inlet. Weller and his team of divers worked many seasons as subcontractors with Mel Fisher who held admiralty claims for many of the 1715 fleet shipwrecks. Each dot on the map marks where a hole was dug with the ship's blower or mailbox.

sailed from Havana in the ill-fated 1715 treasure fleet.

The French captain of *Grifon* had been impatient with Spanish authorities. Captain Antoine d'Aire was not permitted to leave Havana before the treasure fleet left. Authorities took the security precaution to prevent anyone from alerting pirates of the departure of the fleet.

D'Aire was told to remain with the fleet in the convoy. His ship was a faster sailing vessel, and the French captain promptly disobeyed Ubilla's order and set his course for Brest as soon as he could. The *Grifon's* speed proved her

salvation. Captain d'Aire and his vessel arrived in the port of Brest on August 31, 1715. They never knew, until much later, the fate of the Spanish fleet.

With *Grifon* accounted for, treasure salvors working with maritime archaeologists and ship historians have identified the six shipwrecks mentioned here.

- *Nuestra Señora de la Regala San Dimes y San Francisco,* lost near the beach where early treasure hunter Kip Wagner built his cabin, thus called the Cabin Wreck, was General Ubilla's Capitana.

Treasure only dreamed of. Finds in the collection of Bob and Margaret Weller. The Wellers are considered the Deans of the Treasure Divers.

• The *Santo Cristoval de San Roman Nuestra Señora del Rosario y San Jose*, Ubilla's Almiranta, commanded by Admiral de Salmon, was lost off Wabasso Beach and called Corrigan's Wreck by salvors since it is located less than a thousand feet north of property on highway A1A, owned by Hugh Corrigan, who used to find coins washed up on the beach.

• *Nuestra Señora del Carmen San Miguel y San Antonio*, the Capitana of Echeverz's fleet, called the Rio Mar Wreck, was located off the Rio Mar golf course in Vero Beach.

• *The Nuestra Señora del Rosario y San Francisco Xavier*, Echeverz's Almiranta was lost off Sandy Point and called the Sandy Point Wreck by divers.

• Ubilla's *Santissima Trinidad y Nuestra Señora de la Concepcion*, named for her captain and known as the *Urca de Lima* and the Wedge Wreck by divers, was lost just north of the Fort Pierce Inlet and is now a Florida Underwater Archaeological Preserve.

• Ubilla's *Nuestra Señora de las Nieves y las Animas*, lost on the former segregated beach in Fort Pierce south of the inlet, was called the Colored Beach Wreck by early treasure divers. The beach is now named Frederick Douglas Park.

What happened to the other vessels? All were lost in the hurricane—but where? Furious winds turned in a counterclockwise direction from the northwest. As the winds churned around in their hurricane swirl, they caught the fleet near the Florida coastline from the north and east, scattering the vessels onto the reefs and beaches along the coast.

"All of the ships were scattered from the southeast to the northwest," Bob Weller says. "Some of the ships in the 1715 fleet went down in deeper water. We have not yet discovered ballast piles or scatter patterns to account for them."

What happened to the smaller ships in the convoy? What became of the prizes Echeverz captured off Colombia, the naos *San Miguel* and *Concepcion*, the Dutch sloop *Holandesa*, called *Señor de la Popa* by the Spanish, the captured French frigate *El Ciervo*, and Ubilla's small Cuban-made fragatilla?

One vessel that archival records describe as being thrown clear of the water, ended up high and dry on the beach. This ship was the *Señor de la Popa*. It was thrown on the beach south of Vero and used by Echeverz as headquarters.

Survivors from the 136-man crew of the nao *Nuestra Señora de la Concepcion San Jose y San Francisco*, a 265-ton armed cargo ship (with four four-pounder, eighteen ten-pounder, and ten six-pounder iron cannons) ended up on the beach off what is today Cape Canaveral. The

survivors made their way along the beach north to St. Augustine.

Coins discovered by beachcombers on Fernandina Beach south of Nassau Sound have been dated to the time of the 1715 fleet, and there is speculation that the prize ship *San Miguel de Excelsis* may have gone down off shore in the vicinity of Fernandina Beach.

Modern-day salvors have concluded that Ubilla's Cuban frigatilla (called several names, originally the *Maria Galante* and then renamed *Nuestra Señora de la Regala*, adding another "Regala" to the fleet) and the captured French frigate *El Ciervo* sank in very deep water. These two ships remain unaccounted for in the annals of treasure salvage.

When the Spanish received word of the wrecking of the fleet, they dispatched a salvage fleet from Havana to save what they could of the shipwrecked treasure. Some of it was high and dry, stored by surviving crewmen working in an improvised *reale*, or salvage camp, on the beach.

The Spanish salvors established a fort above the dune line to protect their treasure. A raid by the notorious privateer Henry Jennings showed how vulnerable the salvage camp was to attack. The English brigand seized as much treasure as he could carry and fled back to Jamaica in his ship.

The state of Florida built a treasure museum on the very site where the Spanish had their encampment. Visitors to the McLarty Treasure Museum can see artifacts and treasure recovered from the sunken fleet lost virtually on the doorstep.

Spanish salvors of the period labored feverishly. They worked Indian slaves to the point of exhaustion, even death, free diving down into the murky water near shore to bring treasure out of the hulls of sunken ships. By July 1716, Spanish archive records reveal that 5,241,166 pesos worth of silver was recovered. Gold coins and bars were also recovered. The 1715 fleet carried about 14,000,000 pesos in registered gold and silver when it left Havana.

While the Spanish worked the sites methodically to the point of diminishing returns, once they left, minions of treasure seekers tried their hands, diving down to scavenge anything the Spaniards overlooked.

Half of the treasure was never recovered—lost beyond the means of Spanish salvagers to find it, covered over by sand and time, lost to the forces of nature.

"We can never find it all," Bob Weller reminisced with Taffi Fisher Abt, daughter of the legendary Mel Fisher. Taffi sat in a soft leather chair in the Wellers' Lake Worth, Florida, home. She was there to record the oral history of the Wellers' treasure hunting experiences.

"There's always more out there," Margaret Weller smiled as Taffi got out of the chair, stretched, and started to pack up video equipment.

"We need more treasure divers," Taffi said. She was serious. "There are not many of us, and there is a lot to look for." Taffi confirmed her father's hallmark optimism when things looked bleakest—when money was scarce and the treasure boats came back, out of fuel and out of luck. "Today's the day," Mel would exclaim.

Bob and Margaret Weller with some of the treasure they and their teams of divers recovered from Spanish galleons.

Taffi was wearing her dad's slogan on a blue T-shirt. It made Bob Weller smile. "'Today's the day.' That was your dad's thought. 'Follow your dreams' is mine," Bob said.

As far as the 1715 fleet salvage is concerned, no one could have possibly dreamed the legend Bob and Margaret Weller lived to realize—discovery of a king's ransom in treasure under the sea.

The Queen's Jewels, the most amazing gold and diamond jewelry ever recovered from the 1715 fleet. Discovered by Bob and Margaret Weller and their team of divers aboard *Pandion*, a small salvage vessel in which Bob Weller has brought ashore more than $5 million in sunken treasure over the years. It is a very lucky boat.

THE 1733 FLEET

ailing directions were carefully noted on Spanish navigational charts. The perils of the Ocean Sea were well known by 1733, and captains chafed with impatience when they were delayed in Havana. Summer was hurricane season. Gale-force winds were not uncommon, and hurricanes whipped up the Florida Straits at more than a hundred miles an hour.

Rare astrolabe found by the Fishers.

General Rodrigo de Torres y Morales aboard his Capitana *El Rubi* did not know the fate that awaited him when, in the early morning hours of July 13, 1733, the twenty-one ships he commanded sailed past Havana's Fort El Morro while booming cannons saluted their departure. The ships of the New Spain Fleet

were on their way back to Spain. At that very moment in time, hurricane-force winds of 100 miles an hour were churning the water not a hundred miles to the southwest of Key West.

On July 15th, these ships of the New Spain Fleet were caught in that narrow stretch of water between the Bahama Islands to the east and the Florida Keys to the west. There was no escape, with little room to maneuver to seek safety in the open ocean to ride out the storm. The treasure convoy was trapped as high winds from the southeast and heavy seas threw the wooden sailing vessels upon the reefs and shoals of the Florida Keys.

Today, divers and visitors to this narrow spit of coral islands, which stretch from the southern tip of Florida's mainland and follow an arc from Key Biscayne to land's end at Key West, can bear witness to the peril.

Seaward, the ocean is a latticework of shallow coral reefs. Coral mountains rise up underwater and in some places are awash at low tide. Even with carefully marked channels and modern-day charts and navigational systems, ships still ground and wreck on these perilous reefs. Consider, then, the darkness of night hundreds

An aerial photo taken by author from a small plane over the Florida Keys, the site of the wrecking of the 1733 fleet.

of years ago, in the days of the Spanish Main, when ungainly, heavily laden treasure ships were caught in the fury of hurricane winds.

General Morales's own written log records the drama of the destruction of his fleet that sailed from Havana Harbor on July 13, 1733, and wrecked on the reefs and shoals of the Florida Keys:

> *For having arrived at Cayo Largo y Cabeza de los Martires, I fell off to leeward with the fore sail and two spars, governing towards the south, but the heavy wind and seas did not permit us to govern the ship*

well with the bow toward the east, and on the starboard side with the forecastle below the water almost capsizing the vessel.

To be more secure we resolved to change our tack to port. We fought the storm all day until 10 p.m. when we attempted to tack to port more securely, bracing the fore sail all around . . . we ran south until 11 p.m. at which time the sea was so great, and the wind impetuous, forming one great inundation, the wind rising with fierceness producing steep seas. The ship was now unmanageable with the bow toward the east.

The commander of the 1733 treasure fleet went on to write:

> With the starboard rail and forecastle underwater the ship was now in danger of capsizing for being unable to right itself, while at the same time taking many blows from the sea to windward.
>
> It appeared to the head pilot Don Rodrigo de Guerrero, to the ship's captain, and to some other officials that it was necessary to cut away the main mast, which they did. This carried over the mizzenmast, while at the same time the topmast and fore mast fell away, depriving us of all masts. This action served to right the ship somewhat.
>
> The wind finally tore away all the fore sails, even though they were well secured, and the yardarm fell away into the sea. We remained this way helpless in the sea, unable to do more than keep up the work on the pumps and to lighten the between deck spaces of cargo.

Of the twenty-one ships in the treasure fleet, twenty would be disabled, sunk, or grounded on the shoals of the Florida Keys. The cargoes of gold and silver in coin and bullion totaled 12,286,253 pesos.

Smuggled treasure put aboard by dishonest merchants and captains, *sin registrada* (unregistered) to avoid paying the Royal Fifth, amounted to millions of pesos more. Fortunes in jewelry and personal effects of passengers transporting their entire households back to Spain accounted for more wealth than can be contemplated in contemporary value.

THE SPANISH KING'S WARSHIPS

General Don Rodrigo de Torres y Morales had the king's commission to command the treasure fleet when it left Cádiz on August 2, 1732. Don Rodrigo's Capitana or lead ship was officially named *El Rubi Segundo*. Spanish officials were placed aboard *El Rubi* to act as treasurer of the fleet. The Maestre de Plata y Permision was Don Balthesar de la Torre, and the king's representative was Don Alonso Barragan.

These men had their counterparts, minor government officials, put aboard each of the ships in the convoy. The Spanish officials accounted for the cargo and treasure, supervised documentation, and insured not only that the king's treasure was documented but also required that all appropriate taxes had been paid on merchant cargoes.

The Almiranta of the 1733 fleet was the vessel *Nuestra Señora de Balvaneda*—also known as *El Gallo Indiano*, translated "The Cock of the Indies." *El Gallo* sported sixty cannons. It was a Spanish warship in the navy of King Philip V. The *Balvaneda*, or *El Gallo*, was commanded by Captain Bernardo de Maturana.

General Torres, the captain-general, was in overall command of the fleet. The king's admiral, who would oversee the ships and sailors, was aboard the Almiranta, the admiral's ship. Thus the fleet would have at its head the king's lead ship, the Capitana, carrying the general in charge, Don Rodrigo; the last ship in line, the Almiranta, had the commanding admiral aboard.

The vessel *Señor San Joseph*, a sixty-cannon ship, was built in Havana. The ship was new on this voyage and had not been with the fleet that sailed from Cádiz nor with it when treasure was loaded at Veracruz. The vessel was named *El Africa*, and her position in the fleet was the western quarter, to protect the fleet's flank. *El Africa* survived the hurricane, made landfall at Key Largo, and sailed for Spain on July 24, arriving in Cádiz on September 25, 1733. *El Africa* carried no treasure aboard; only tobacco.

The *Nuestra Señora de Balvaneda* bore the same official name as the Almiranta and was therefore was nicknamed *El Infante*. This was the fourth warship of the crown in the fleet. Constructed in 1724, in Genoa, the armed merchant ship was designed to carry treasure from the New World back to Spain. The outward-bound cargo was mercury used to refine silver. The hull was sheathed to prevent teredo worms from boring into the wood in the tropical seas. *El Infante* carried sixty cannons to protect the fleet in the event of attack.

A *pink* or *pinque*, called *Nuestra Señora del Populo*, an armed vessel owned by the king, was captained by Don Francisco Imbernon.

THE MERCHANT VESSELS

The rest of the ships in the convoy were of various origins and construction. These privately owned merchant ships were licensed to trade with the Indies and carry goods back to Spain. The ships were:

- The nao *San Felipe*, called *El Lerri*, owned by the Marques de Canada.

- *El Gran Poder de Dios y Santa Ana*, or simply *Anna Augustina*, a merchant ship.

- The merchant ship *San Pedro*.

- The *San Jose de las Animas*, a merchant ship simply called *San Jose*.

- *Nuestra Señora de las Angustias y San Raphael*, a merchant ship owned by Jose Sanchez de Madrid.

- The merchant ship *Nuestra Señora del Rosario, San Antonio y San Vicente Ferrer* owned by Don Jacinto de Arizon and captained by Juan Jose de Arizon, thus called the *Sueco de Arizon* for short.

- *San Francisco de Asis*, an English-built merchant ship.

- *San Ignacio*, a nao or merchant ship.

- *Nuestra Señora del Carmen San Antonio de Padua y las Animas*, owned and captained by Don Antonio de Chavez, thus called *Sueco de Chavez*, a Genoese-built merchant ship, called a nao.

- *Nuestra Señora de Belen y San Antonio de Padua*, an English-built merchant ship owned and captained by Don Luis de Herrera, thus called the *Sueco de Herrera*.

Diver Brad Johnson holding emerald-studded gold piece of jewelry he found on Treasure Beach. Nearby, the *El Lerri* broke apart in the 1733 hurricane.

- *Nuestra Señora de los Dolores y Santa Isabel*, called the *Tres Puentes* (meaning three decks).

- *Nuestra Señora del Rosario y Santo Domingo*.

- *Nuestra Señora de los Reyes San Fernando y San Francisco de Padua*.

- The French-built *Nuestra Señora del Rosario San Francisco Javier y San Antonio de Padua*.

- The nao *Nuestra Señora de Belen y San Juan Bautista*.

- A frigate, the *Fragata de Florida*.

- *La Balandrita*, a balandra or schooner.

SPANISH SALVAGE OF THE FLEET

What is known for certain is that the New Spain Fleet left Cádiz on August 2, 1732, and arrived in Veracruz in October. Cargoes were off-loaded and treasure and goods taken on for the eventual voyage back to Spain after the ships were refitted.

It was an unhealthy season on the Mexican coast. Spaniards paid little attention to sanitary

Aerial view of the Florida Keys. The man-made canal was cut through coral to provide access for boats. It is apparent that when Spanish galleons came ashore here in 1733, they would have struck the reefs and been dashed to pieces by the fury of the hurricane.

conditions in the shantytowns that were thrown up at what became annual trade fairs when the fleet arrived. Many Spaniards died of cholera.

Normally the fleet would leave Veracruz in April for Havana, then head back to Spain well before the summer of storms in the tropics.

The mule trains of La Plata, carrying coins from the mint in Mexico City and bullion from Mexican silver mines, were late. Once the silver and gold were stowed, fresh fruits and vegetables were loaded last to keep them from spoiling. It was a slow process.

The trip across the Gulf of Mexico to Havana usually took merchant ships three weeks. The 1733 fleet left Veracruz on May 25, 1733, and were recorded arriving in Havana from June 24th to 26th, 1733. Don Rodrigo sailed *El Rubi* out of Havana on July 13, 1733.

If there had been satellite images of weather patterns available then, the navigators would have known, at that very moment in time, the fury of a hurricane was building southeast and heading toward Cuba and the Florida Straits.

It was the worst possible time for ships to be caught in the narrow Bahamas Channel. Every ship would be wrecked or severely damaged, thrown up on the Florida Keys. Only the Cuban-built *El Africa* that ran far west for flank protection was saved by the swift Gulf Stream that pushed it out of harm's way. *El Africa* survived, but not without damage.

The deposition of Francisco de Varas y Valdez, *El Africa's* lieutenant, documented the events aboard ship:

[The fleet] proceeded to the entrance of the Canal of the Bahamas and on the night of the 14th there came upon them a storm out of the north of such qualities that at 2 a.m. this ship was forced before it, without having seen any other ship of the convoy since midnight. At 11 a.m. of the next day, and within two hours, they lost the main mid mast and mizzen topmast. At 6 p.m. the wind came upon them very strong from the south, which lasted all the following night. At daybreak on the 16th it started to calm. By jury-rigging the fore mast sail they made their way to Key Largo where the currents were less severe and they anchored with two anchors in 40 brazas of water. . . . They discovered on the 17th two lost ships, and after awhile were able to launch a boat to the water to go out and reconnoiter them. The ships were found to be the pink *of His Majesty named* El Populo, *and the advice ship of the council whose people they picked up around it on the said day, and the following day, and conducted them on board their ship. Immediately they started jury-rigging the ship to be able to resume navigation. On the 24th of July they made sail from the mentioned site of Key Largo and proceeded on their voyage to Spain."*

El Africa arrived in Cádiz on September 24, 1733.

After the 1733 treasure fleet left Havana, heavy rain and high winds lashed the island of Cuba. Boats that set out after the departure of Don Rodrigo's fleet returned to port. Cuba's governor, the Marques de Cavesas, sent a small ship out once the hurricane-force winds abated to search for the treasure fleet. Meanwhile another ship returned to Cuba, having been forced back in its voyage. That vessel had sailed out on July 18, 1733, and found twelve ships of the fleet grounded upon the Florida Keys.

The Cuban governor reacted immediately. Upon receiving the news from this ship that returned to Havana, de Cavesas sent out nine salvage vessels. The Cuban governor's report dated August 18, 1733, described his actions at the time: "I promptly prepared nine balandras [ships] with provisions, divers, munitions, gunners, a company of Grenadiers with all its officials, and the shipbuilder Don Juan Acosta. I gave them instructions for the securing of treasure which is to be remitted to this Plaza, and principally from the English city of Providence which, when learning of this will approach with some wreckers."

Salvage of the Spanish treasure fleet was begun almost at once. Survivors in the beached vessels, under the direction of captains and officers, began to set up camps on the Keys. The Spanish organized a base camp on Mata Cumbe Grande, which is today Islamorada. Other salvage camps were located on Indian Key, Long Key, and Grassy Key. The line of

Good example of a cob coin struck by hand with dies. The piece of eight was clipped to the proper weight, then struck.

wrecked ships stretched for some thirty-six miles all along the beaches and shallows.

Many of the vessels could be salvaged. Provisions were taken from ship's stores to supply the survivors and workers with food and fresh drinking water. The little cargo vessel that was destined to bring 256 barrels of flour from Cuba to St. Augustine, Florida, remained intact, and the survivors used the flour. Launches and one of the small courier ships were refitted and used by the shipwrecked sailors to sail along the coast and carry news and supplies to the salvage camps.

The salvage vessels from Cuba arrived on the scene. The commander of the nine ships in the rescue party, Juan Thomas de la Herrera, wrote "This prompt aid and the forty divers which were sent in these rescue ships was the major alleviation of those that were shipwrecked. The first thing done was to commence the underwater search which was executed with all effort, salvaging all the treasure from the Capitana, Almiranta and the refuerzo."

This report revealed that cargoes of treasure from the *El Rubi*, *El Gallo Indiano*, and *Nuestra Señora de Balvaneda*, known as *El Infante*, were salvaged immediately.

The salvage operation became a well-organized undertaking. Armed ships set up patrols; divers and salvors from Cuba followed

The bronze marker for 1733 fleet, seen from Route 1.

orders of salvage masters and officials appointed to account for the treasure. The long line of sunken ships had to be protected from pirates and unauthorized salvage; infrastructure of the salvage camps was organized to victualize and pay salvors for their work.

The importance of archive research was apparent when Bob Weller, a pioneer diver who began diving the remnants of the 1733 fleet in 1960, said, "The aviso was salvaged. It was pulled off the reef and refloated. Letters from Don Rodrigo show that he was able to refit the aviso and use it to carry water. A lot of people looked for the aviso one mile south of *El Populo*. If they did proper research, they would have saved themselves a lot of trouble."

The Spanish accounted for all of the treasure they recovered from the 1733 fleet. Scribes recorded amounts paid to the salvors. Minute details appear in Spanish archives, for example: 592 copper ingots mined in Cuba were aboard *El Rubi*. Only eight were not recovered. *El Gallo* had 517 copper ingots on the ship's manifest and salvors recovered 438. Cannons listed as being salvaged and freighted to Havana totaled 670.

Tax records reveal the meticulous accounting for cargoes of specie and bullion as well as silver wares and general cargo. The manifests revealed 12,286,253 pesos of gold and silver when the ships loaded the treasure on board at Veracruz. The Spanish recorded that 12,281,500 pesos of coins were recovered from the three principal ships *El Rubi, El Gallo,* and *Nuestra Señora de Balvaneda (El Infante).*

Sin registrada (unregistered) gold and silver contraband was recovered that accounted for 236,247 pesos from the *San Joseph y las Animas,* nicknamed the *San Jose.* Fifty-four thousand pesos of sin registrada specie and bullion were salvaged from the *San Ignacio.* This meant that 285,494 pesos of contraband above the manifested cargo escaped the king's tax collectors.

Spanish reales, the name used for salvage camps, were set up and continued to recover treasure from the shipwrecks for a year after their loss on the Florida Keys. For recoveries that could not easily be made by off-loading cargoes from flooded holds of grounded ships, the Spanish used Indian free divers who swam down into the clear water and brought up treasure. In 1734, the salvors burned some of the ships and removed the iron that could be salvaged.

What remained along the coast were piles of ballast stones that followed the outline of the ship's hulls. A treasure trove of personal wealth of passengers traveling back to Spain with all of their worldly goods and a fortune in treasure that was not salvaged, eventually forgotten to time and the tides, was covered over by shifting sands.

MODERN SALVAGE

Contemporary salvage divers of the twentieth century who explored the shipwreck remains of the fleet of 1733 that were left as piles of ballast stones in the shape of a vessel had difficulty identifying particular vessels unless an item of property, a marked cannon, or definitive evidence was located on the site.

The Spanish made charts in 1733, showing approximate positions where the vessels wrecked. The charts were not easy to use for modern salvagers. The positions were vague and the names of keys changed, as did landmarks and the topography of the islands in the chain.

Modern salvage divers began finding treasure almost by accident. "Art McKee started it," Bob Weller recounted the story of early salvage of the 1733 shipwrecks. "He was a hard hat diver. He was going along the outer edge of the reef looking for bronze and copper to sell as scrap metal. He could pick up a bronze spike or pin that weighed twenty pounds, that was a good day's work," Weller said.

El Rubi

"McKee was the manager of the Homestead City swimming pool. One day Reggie Roberts, a commercial fisherman, stopped by to see Art. 'If you're looking for iron, there's a pile of rocks in the Keys with a bunch of cannon. If you're interested in iron, I'll take you,' Reggie told McKee," Bob Weller related the story of how Art McKee began going out on Reggie's boat.

"One weekend Art went diving. He took his Miller-Dunn diving helmet. When he went down, he saw a big pile of rocks. Cannons were all around," Weller related.

"McKee said, 'This doesn't look anything like a shipwreck.' That's how Art got started. He dove on the Capitana," Weller said.

The Art McKee Treasure Museum in the Florida Keys.

"Art wanted to protect the site so [he] applied for a lease from the state of Florida. They gave him a lease five miles by five miles, which included the Capitana, the *San Pedro*, *El Infante*. The area encompassed the *San Jose* but nobody knew it," Weller laughed.

Weller was Art McKee's biographer. His book *Galleon Hunt* details the early days of McKee's salvage diving in the Florida Keys. Bob was later to dive on many of the wreck sites of the 1733 fleet and make his own fabulous finds.

"Art was finding so much on the Capitana that he paid no attention to the *San Pedro* or *Infante*," Weller said. He leaned back in his chair, a broad smile crossed his face as he put both hands behind his head and began to relate the famous standoff between Art McKee and men McKee considered pirates on his treasure site.

"In 1959, Tim Watkins and six other divers began working the *Infante* site from their salvage boat *Buccaneer*," Bob Weller said. He pushed himself back in his swivel chair and began to relish the tale of piracy and high adventure.

"They found a gold coin, a lot of silver coins, swords, plates. There was a picture of them on the *Buccaneer* coming up the Miami River after an excursion working the *Infante* site holding a rapier and arquebus. They worked the *Infante* like Grant worked Richmond," Weller laughed as he remembered the incident.

"The *Buccaneer* crew only worked the ballast pile. They thought everything was in the ballast pile. We all thought that at the time. So they missed a lot. From the *Infante* they went to the Capitana. I was down there when they were out on the Capitana and had a face-off with Art McKee. The famous underwater standoff on the ballast pile of the Capitana." Weller related the story of how volatile tempers became when treasure was involved.

"Art had a bang stick. All these divers came down from the *Buccaneer* with spear guns. At the time Art had the ribs of the ship sticking up to show tourists when he'd take them out to the site. The divers took the bang stick from Art and hit one of the ship's ribs with it. It exploded. They got all scared and went up, all except Jimmy Green, who finally went up. Jimmy is the only one who is still alive today from the *Buccaneer* crew of seven. This standoff made the news," Weller recalled.

"That's when the state of Florida said to Art, 'We can't protect you. You're outside the three-mile limit of state territorial waters. You figure it out.' The state really had no interest," Weller said.

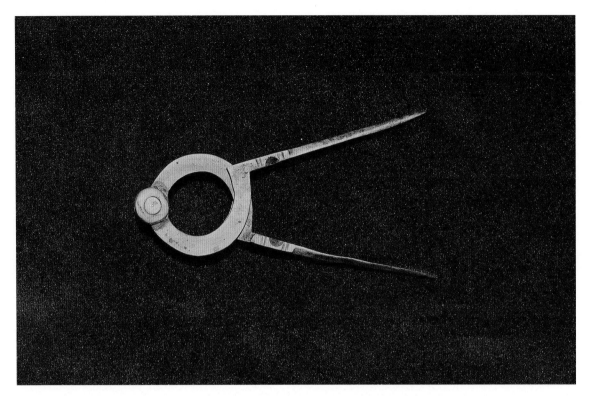

Brass navigational dividers from a 1733 shipwreck. Dividers have not changed in basic design over the centuries. They are used for marking out distance on nautical charts.

The last thing the treasure salvors needed was heat from authorities or serious feuds between them that would be carried in the press. "Kip Watson, the captain of the *Buccaneer*, went down and cooled things down. It was a tempest in a teapot. They didn't want to get the state all riled up, and I think they ran out of money at the time. That was 1960, and I arrived." Weller was enjoying the recollection of these early days of treasure salvage in the Florida Keys.

The stage was set for other salvors to begin a systematic hunt for treasure from the 1733 fleet. "By 1960, Art had given up on the Capitana because of the Watson-*Buccaneer* group conflict. He was actively looking for the *Gen-*

ovesa on the Pedro Banks about ninety miles south of Jamaica. When I came on the scene, I became the fourth active salvage group working the 1733 fleet. There was Bobby Klein, Craig Hamilton, Art Sapp, and us, the Bob Weller group. The next year Marty Meylach got involved. He was the fifth group," Weller related.

"The key to this whole thing . . ." Weller paused in his recollection. He looked around his office at a box frame that displayed antique Spanish navigational dividers he recovered from shipwrecks. The pause created a detour as Weller described his meeting with Craig Hamilton.

Weller was out on his boat working a site in the keys. "The marine patrol stopped and

Iron cannons in the Keys.

asked me what we're finding. I said some bronze pins. The marine patrol said 'Guys over there are finding coins,'" Weller recalled.

"I went over and there were two boats anchored over the *Infante*. I introduced myself and met Craig Hamilton. He invited me aboard for a cup of coffee. Craig was diving on the *Infante*. Once we got to know each other, Craig took me under his wing," Weller said.

"The HMS *Fly* sank in this area in 1805," Weller said. Weller and his former professor at the University of Delaware, Dr. Harry Wiseman, had formed a friendship that lasted long after Weller graduated. Wiseman got a job teaching at the University of Miami and moved

to Florida. The two men went out salvaging together. They were together the day they met Craig Hamilton.

"We dived seaward of the *Infante* on the HMS *Fly* and found a glass prism and bronze hinge off Little Conch Reef where it sank," Weller said. Weller wanted to know more about the HMS *Fly*. "I wrote the British Museum of History about the *Fly*. They sent me a list of charts. One stood out; it was of the 1733 Spanish plate fleet. I called the museum. A woman I spoke to told me it would cost me to get the charts. I asked how much," Weller smiled.

"The woman at the British Museum said the charts would cost fifty cents. I told her I'd send her five dollars and asked her to rush the charts to me. She sent five charts by the British and Spanish of the salvage of the 1733 fleet and a manifest of what each ship contained." Weller's enthusiasm was evident as he recalled his early days of treasure hunting when everything found belonged to the finders, before government regulations hampered their efforts.

Weller had been invited to Craig Hamilton's home. Craig showed him what they had been recovering from the sunken ships. The men became friends. Weller brought the charts over to show Craig.

Weller took up the story: "Craig Hamilton and I put a chart on the table. Craig got out an old pair of Spanish navigational dividers to measure distance. We noticed on the first chart, around the north end of Islamorada called Upper Matecumbe Key, that all the Keys were shown. The reason for this was that General Rodrigo de Torres y Morales had his reale, or salvage camp, there on the north end of Matecumbe Grande," Weller said.

"That's where the Chesapeake Restaurant is today on Islamorada. On the west side of A1A is where Rodrigo set up four cannons and built a fort. You can still see a depression where the cannons were," Weller detoured again.

"That's where he had his reale. They marked the reefs in there so ships coming to pick up silver from Havana wouldn't hit the reef. The chart showed Dove Key and Rodrigo Island. The important thing was, Craig and I said then, in order to get an idea of distance accurately to be able to find the sites marked on the old charts, we had to know the distance used on the chart.

"The Spanish knew the distance accurately from Dove Key to Rodrigo Island. It was a league or just under three miles. Once we had our idea of distance, we could go down the chart and start naming the keys," Weller said.

This proved to be a crucial piece in the puzzle to locate just where the ships of the 1733 fleet were grounded. In many cases their wooden members were burned to the water line by Spanish salvors and any timbers that remained that were not buried deep under the sand had long ago been eaten by teredo worms.

"That was the key to start unlocking the box, the turning point of the 1733 salvage effort. We were able to get an idea on which Key each ship sank. Once we were able to do that, it was a lot easier to go out and locate each wreck, and we knew the name of each ship, which was important," Weller said.

The divers were discovering a new shipwreck every four months or so. "Each ship had its own story," Weller said.

El Infante

The site Bob Weller cut his teeth on in the Florida Keys was the *Nuestra Señora de Balvaneda*, known as *El Infante. El Infante* was a heavily armed warship with sixty cannons. It measured some 120 feet long with a width of 38 feet, displaced 400 tons. The ship, built in Genoa in 1724, had double-hull planking to protect it from teredo worms in the tropical seas of the New World. *El Infante* was one of the four warships King Philip V of Spain sent with Don Rodrigo in the 1733 fleet to Veracruz.

El Infante transported mercury used to refine silver, a commodity the crown carefully monitored and monopolized. It was a control over illegal silver production and smuggling. As would be apparent when the 1733 fleet was salvaged, smuggling of contraband silver and gold had become a well-practiced art by the time the 1733 fleet set sail from Havana. Beside its cargo of mercury, other trade goods were also off-loaded from *El Infante* in Veracruz.

El Infante, like the other ships in the 1733 Nueva España Fleet, anchored off Veracruz and took on silver that was transported by mule trains from Mexico City. The Spanish scribes carefully recorded the cargo put aboard the king's ship: 186 boxes of silver coins with 3,000 coins to the box to total 558,000 pesos, as well as cochineal dye, leather hides, Chinese porcelain wares, wood, and local wares.

El Infante sailed with the rest of Don Rodrigo's fleet from Veracruz for the month-long voyage to Havana. Their late arrival, on June 25, 1733, sealed the fate of the convoy, which would leave Cuba in the throes of hurricane season.

The log of *El Infante* for the entry of July 15, 1733 reads in part: "The ship was now opening up between decks, further filling the hold with water . . . at 6 p.m. the wind changed to the south with as much, if not more, violence than before, the blows of the seas always continuing to add to our torment and we continuously worked at the pumps to keep the ship afloat. At 8:30 p.m. the ship struck bottom and continued doing so for a quarter of an hour with horrendous blows, taking on water fast."

The ship's log for July 16th described the aftermath of the hurricane. "At daybreak the weather was clear and we could see the land and with the light of day we could see the coast of the northeast-southwest which we recognized as the beginning of the Key Largo at the entrance to the Canal of the Bahamas, about two leagues distant."

Rafts were made to take passengers and crew ashore as the survivors now saw that other ships in the convoy were grounded on the reefs nearby. By July 23rd, the *Infante's* log records that salvage was underway. "The *buceo* (diving) of the Capitana commences this day and continues with good results."

The notation in *Infante's* log for August 4th reads: "We received notice that all the silver had been taken off the Almiranta and taken ashore." The report in the log for August 7th recorded: "The ship *Murgia* (*Nuestra Señora del Rosario y Santo Domingo*) was off-loaded and is now afloat awaiting the trip to Havana. The buceo of the *Infante* started this day and was finished on the 9th, having salvaged 180 boxes of silver coins, lacking just six from concluding the registry."

The Spanish scribes noted that 568,613 pesos of silver coins were recovered from the 558,000 loaded aboard in Veracruz. Satisfied with their work, the Spanish salvors burned ships to recover fastenings and to clear the coast so unwanted looters could not benefit from the spoils left behind on the Keys.

What Bob Weller and his friends found when he first dove the site of *El Infante* on Little Conch Reef was a pile of ballast rocks, smooth river rocks, put into the deep hold over the keel to give sailing vessels stability. Art McKee had worked the *Infante* but was more interested in the gold he was recovering from *El Rubi*, the Capitana.

What salvage divers eventually realized was that a lot of cargo, including the effects of passengers, scattered away from the wreckage with the force of the hurricane. The result was the recovery of many gold coins, artifacts, and silver coins—including rare pillar dollars dated 1732 and 1733.

McKee built a museum around 1956. It looked like a fortress surrounded by a moat on Plantation Key. It became a tourist attraction. The McKees took visitors out to the site four miles directly off the museum building and offered tours of the treasure museum.

The *San Pedro*

Meanwhile other salvors kept locating ballast piles. The *San Pedro's* remains were spotted off a small island called Indian Key. It became a going enterprise for salvage divers to take tourists with them. The tourists would pay for the fuel and lunch, and the salvors would have time on site. The *San Pedro* was yielding small denomination cob coins.

Bob Weller was working as an engineer for the Honeywell Corporation at the time, so he could only dive on weekends. His pal Craig Hamilton told him about the finds on the *San Pedro* and Weller joined him. When Weller joined in the venture, the *San Pedro* ballast pile was intact. The salvors had cut holes down to the coral rock off the main ballast pile.

Craig Hamilton and another salvor, Bobby Klein, recovered a whole sack of small denomination silver cob coins. "They brought up 8,000 in one day," Bob Weller exclaimed.

Weller found fifty small denomination one- and two-reale silver coins. The silver was likely the horde of the *San Pedro's* owner who sold his cargo of European trade goods for 16,000 pesos in the small denomination silver coins Weller and the salvage divers had been finding.

The *San Pedro* also loaded Chinese porcelain wares that had reached Veracruz by mule trains. The porcelain carried included delicate Chinese cups, saucers, and bowls. Oriental wares came all across Mexico from Spain's galleons that traded with the Philippines and from there with traders on the coast of China.

The *San Pedro* grounded, and water flooded its hull. Spanish salvors recovered most of *San Pedro's* cargo. Bob Weller assumed that the bag of small denomination silver coins recovered by the salvage divers may have fallen into the water during salvage attempts, since cargo and coins were taken by launch to Indian Key.

Today, the *San Pedro* has been named a Florida Underwater Archaeological Preserve. The shipwreck can be visited by divers but cannot be disturbed in any way. The state has placed concrete cannons around the *San Pedro's* ballast pile and an anchor near the site, which consists of a ninety-foot-long by thirty-foot-wide stone ballast pile.

Divers can see flat, red ladrillo bricks among the ballast stones. The bricks were part of the ship's galley oven. The shipwreck preserve of the *San Pedro* is located 1.25 nautical miles south of Indian Key in about eighteen feet of water.

Salvage in the Florida Keys provided humor and disappointment, camaraderie and conflict. In the beginning, state authorities were not interested, and the salvage divers had unfettered access to the shipwrecks. Art McKee obtained leases to sites that covered vast areas that he could never exploit in his lifetime. Once treasure finds of gold and silver began to surface and news reports aired about the fabulous treasure being found in the Keys, Florida officials changed their tune.

The *San Jose*

Bob Weller began a search for the *San Jose y las Animas*, called simply *San Jose*. The 326-ton vessel was christened *Saint Joseph* and sold to a Spaniard, Don Joseph del Duque, who renamed the vessel *San Jose y las Animas*, Saint Joseph and the Spirits. "We dragged around a long time looking for the *San Jose*," Weller said. "We couldn't find it. Tom Gurr found it. Gurr worked the *San Jose* twice. The first time the state threatened him. Gurr got so angry he arranged for television to come down. Tom dumped the treasure back into the ocean on the *San Jose* site in front of the TV cameras. He made quite a name for himself," Weller said.

Weller remembered the incident with a smile. At the time it wasn't funny, since it marked a point in time when there was confrontation rather than cooperation between treasure divers and the state of Florida.

"Tom Gurr sank about three barrels of treasure. Gurr loaded it in his sixteen-foot lapstrake boat that took a wave and flooded with water in front of the rolling television news cameras," Weller said. "We looked for Gurr's lapstrake boat but couldn't find it," he added.

The *San Jose* joined Don Rodrigo's fleet in Cádiz. It traded for 30,435 pesos in silver, carried K'ang Hsi Chinese porcelains, cacao, vanilla, cochineal, hides, and other general cargo. "The coins smuggled aboard as contraband were ten times what was on the *San Jose's* manifests," Bob Weller said.

The Weller collection of treasure recovered from sunken Spanish shipwrecks includes some fine examples of porcelain from Chingtechen, Kiangsi province. The Chinese had developed an elaborate firing system for their porcelain wares and decorated them with patterns applied by artisans. Chinese packed the porcelain in straw and sent it to the port of Nanking where junks would take it to the Philippines. It was sold for gold and silver to the Spanish who controlled the Manila trade.

Spanish Manila galleons took as long as half-a-year to reach Acapulco on Mexico's Pacific coast where the fragile cargoes were transported across Mexico to be loaded on vessels of the annual plate fleet back to Spain. *San Jose's* cargo of porcelains was a treasure trove for early salvage divers.

Documents in the Archives of the Indies in Seville record the sinking of the *San Jose*: "The navio of *El Duque* flooded immediately upon grounding, and its officials, passengers, soldiers, and sailors sought shelter on the roundhouse. All were saved on rafts." Being saved did not mean being forgiven by the crown, since the merchants pleaded with Don Rodrigo for dispensation for smuggling 236,247 pesos of silver aboard *San Jose*.

"The *San Jose* wasn't burned by Spanish salvors since it grounded and sank back in deeper water. The ship just disintegrated in time," Bob Weller explained.

The *San Jose's* lead-sheathed rudder was torn away when the ship grounded in the shallows. The rudder and cannons were found by diver Tom Gurr who took the Smithsonian Institution's maritime historian Mendel Peterson aboard his salvage ship to participate and map the excavation of the *San Jose*.

A lead water pump was found on the *San Jose* site with a date: 1728. The ship was built around that time in the colonies of New England by British shipwrights.

Silver plates recovered, bearing an English maker's mark, provided evidence that the divers were on the New England–made *Saint Joseph*. Amazing finds of ivory-handled razors, combs, and K'ang Hsi wares were found along with small pottery figures.

Bob Weller joined Tom Gurr aboard Gurr's salvage vessel the *Parker*. Newspaper reports brought Gurr into conflict with the state of Florida. Gurr insisted that the *San Jose* was in international waters some 4.8 miles offshore, well beyond the three-mile state territorial limit that would have required him to obtain a lease to work the site.

Tom Gurr was arrested by the sheriff of Monroe County and charged with illegally sal-

vaging artifacts. Florida claimed that the barrier reef offshore was what set its territorial limit, not the shoreline.

The legal maneuvering and associated costs took all of Tom Gurr's financial resources. The state of Florida confiscated artifacts that Gurr had recovered, and subsequent negotiations found state officials stone-walling the hapless salvor who had been allowed to resume salvage work and was beginning to uncover gold coins, jewelry, and newly minted pillar dollars.

It was then that Gurr dumped treasure back on the *San Jose* site. The televised account and Gurr's heated comments about the state's unfairness got him arrested again. State officials searched a canal behind his house and found some artifacts.

Henry Taylor, a former beer distributor from Delaware who had moved to the Keys, was working on treasure projects with Mel Fisher. He put together what he called the "Salt Watergate" legal defense fund for Tom Gurr.

In a story right out of the movies, the Salt Watergate defense team tried to sell coins to raise money for Tom Gurr's legal defense. A "meet" was apparently set up with an inside operative working for the Florida Department of Law Enforcement (FDLE). When the gold was gathered at the meeting place, FDLE officers came in and seized the coins, stating they were from the *San Jose*.

Henry Taylor was cut out of salvage rights by the state of Florida—retaliation for taking Gurr's side. Gurr was threatened and his wife was threatened with prosecution for being an accomplice to grand larceny. Gurr was broke, and the threats forced him to plead guilty to grand larceny in state court in Key West. He received two years probation.

Gurr was vindicated a year later when the U.S. Supreme Court ruled that the state of Florida had no claim to the shipwrecks beyond the three-mile limit. The *San Jose* was ruled to be beyond that three-mile limit.

For the young treasure hunter, the justification came only after years of heartbreak and unfair treatment at the hands of Florida state officials who eventually dissipated artifacts that he found and never properly accounted for their misconduct, having used their power to distort the law for their own greed and jealousy.

El Populo

When Bob Weller began work on the 1733 fleet in the Keys, many ships in the treasure fleet had not been discovered. "Up until 1967, the *Populo, San Jose, San Fernando,* and *Ignacio* were four missing ships. We didn't know it then, but Carl Frederick, Carl Ward, Bob McKay, and Lee Harding had found the *Populo* and were salvaging it undercover. They left a cannon on it. Word leaked out," Bob Weller recalled the events.

"Marty Meylach [a fellow diver] went out to the site. When the group came back and saw that the cannon was missing, they stopped salvaging it. *El Populo* sank up against a reef in twenty-eight feet of water. The Spanish were able to salvage a lot of it," Weller said. "There wasn't a lot on it to begin with."

Nuestra Señora del Populo was a pinque or pink, the name for smaller warships that could also run faster and take on some cargo. The *Populo*, the property of the Royal Hacienda, may have been 150 tons and likely shipped eight cannons. Spanish archives record that *El Populo* took on indigo, cochineal, leather hides, K'ang Hsi Chinese porcelains, and fruits in Veracruz and tobacco in Havana. Treasure would have been the personal property of the ship's officers and crew.

The small pinque was shoved far north by the fury of the hurricane. It ended up to be the northernmost vessel that struck the Keys. With its hull holed by coral reefs, the little ship sank and remained underwater with part of its deck awash at high tide. None of the ship's crew was lost, but its cargo was underwater.

Nearby was the little *El Aviso* that did not sink, although it was dismasted. The *Aviso* sent its launch to bring the *Populo's* crew aboard, and together they sought shelter on the Keys. It was *El Africa*, the only ship in the convoy to survive the hurricane, that spotted the two ships. *El Africa's* captain sent a boat to search for the crews and took them aboard.

"The *El Africa* sailed back to Spain with the survivors of the *Aviso* and *El Populo* without realizing the other ships had sunk," Weller said.

Tres Puentes

Weller described how his friends decided to fly a small plane over the area to try and locate the remaining ships. From the air it would be easy to see the outline of ballast piles in clear Keys water.

"Sunday Don Gurgiola, Art Sapp, Marty Meylach, and John Knox decided to go up in Don Gurgiola's four seat Seabee pusher-prop plane. *Herrera* (*Nuestra Señora de Belen y San Antonio de Padua* owned and captained by Don Luis de Herrera) had already been found. We knew the *Herrera* was close to the *Tres Puentes* (*Nuestra Señora de los Dolores y Santa Isabel*)," Weller related.

"Marty Meylach was down from Miami. He sat in the back seat. There was a rivalry of course between salvors. They started taxiing across the bay. The plane had to reach ninety miles an hour to take off. The pilot teased Marty who was nervous in the plane.

"Don't know if we can get over the mangroves," Don the pilot jibed as the plane held the water before lifting off. Mangroves on the other side of the bay loomed closer and closer. "Marty was in a panic. Of course the pilot had taken off in that bay many times and knew he'd make it.

"They were about to call it a day when one of the men looked down and saw a gray spot against the reef. They dropped a buoy on it. The pilot turned to Marty and asked him if he wanted to stay over in the Keys and go out with the small group to check on the site. Marty was gruff and replied, 'No that's not the *Tres Puentes*.'" Weller recounted. Marty returned to his home in Miami.

"The next day Art Sapp and Don Gurgiola went out to where they had dropped the buoy from the plane. They took a spear and pushed it into the sand. It went clunk and they knew they were on ballast stones," Weller said.

"When Don and Art finished salvaging the *Tres Puentes*, Meylach went in. Marty went fifteen feet from where they had been working and found silver wedges. He never told anyone how many he found," Weller added.

Tres Puentes, Three Decks in Spanish, was officially the *Nuestra Señora de los Dolores y Santa Isabel*. It was built in England and displaced 296 tons. Spanish archive records revealed that the *Tres Puentes* loaded 20,000 pesos in treasure at Veracruz along with the dyes of indigo and cochineal, hides, sugar, and brasilwood.

The Spanish salvors recovered 13,098 pesos of silver from the *Tres Puentes*, but, according to Bob Weller, very little other treasure was recovered from the wreck site, making him conclude that the hurricane scattered the wreckage over a larger area.

El Sueco de Arizon & the San Francisco

Bob was finding a lot of coins working the *Nuestra Señora del Rosario San Antonio San Vicente Ferrer*, a merchant vessel owned by Don Jacinto de Arizon. It was called for short *El Sueco de Arizon*. In the midst of that work Bob Weller discovered the *San Francisco* almost by accident. The *San Francisco* was the short name of the *Nuestra Señora del Rosario San Francisco Javier y San Antonio de Padua*. It was a merchant nao.

Weller described his discovery: "When I found the *San Francisco*, we were working the *Sueco de Arizon*. We would come under Long Key Bridge to get out to the *Sueco* by Dutch Key. There were clues that I missed. The biggest clue was a photograph of salvage diver

Tim Watkins standing on the dock with twenty-seven copper discs. There were only two ships carrying copper disks from Cuba; they were the Almiranta and Capitana.

"While we worked the *Sueco* on Columbus Day, there was a fishing tournament going on, and the channel going under the bridge was full of anchored boats. That day, instead of stirring up fishing lines, I took the next bridge north," Weller said.

"That is the north end of Craig Key. When I came around that channel and out around the edge of the reef, I spotted a ballast pile. The ballast pile was probably a half-mile from the Almiranta and lay in eight feet of water. I told the other three divers in the boat. 'There's a ballast pile there,' and asked them if they wanted to take a look. The answer was no. We were finding coins on the *Sueco*. At 3 p.m. we came back, and I decided to look at the ballast pile," Weller related.

"I started to work the seaward end of the ballast pile. The first thing I found was a piece of blue and white K'ang Hsi Chinese porcelain." Weller told the tale of his dramatic and serendipitous discovery.

"I was working as a fifty-fifty subcontractor on the *Sueco* with Mel Fisher. I'd promised Mel that I'd call him every night and tell him what I found. Up until that time Mel's group, Armada Research, had found twenty-seven wrecks but no treasure—treasure we were picking up from *Sueco* was icing on the cake," Weller smiled.

Weller called Fisher. "I mentioned to Mel I found an unworked ballast pile and that I knew it was from the 1733 fleet, because I

Bob Weller with a Chinese porcelain cup.

found a piece of K'ang Hsi on it. Tony Clausen, it was Carl Clausen but we called him Big Tony, was the state archaeologist. When I called Mel in Fort Pierce, Tony Clausen was there. Mel turned around and told Tony, 'It looks like Bob found another 1733 wreck,'" Weller related.

"My salvage boat was called the *Big Fisherman*, docked at Greyhound Key, now called

Fiesta Key. Next morning when we pulled up to load our gear on board, there sat Tony and Mel Fisher," Weller said.

"Tony said, 'Bob, take me out to your new wreck.' I should have told him to go pound sand," Weller shook his head, remembering the prelude to years of frustration that would follow.

"I took Mel and Tony out to the wreck site along with my divers, and we worked it for a couple of hours. Tony found a silver fork in the ballast pile. I found some cannon balls," Weller related the incident.

"Tony said, 'All right take me back to the dock.' We got to the dock and Tony said, 'Bob you know this is a 1733 wreck site and you don't have a lease on it, so I want you to stay off it.'"

"At that time we were rolling in coins on the *Sueco*, so we didn't go back to it. I found the wreck in 1966. The wreck stayed there, nobody touched it. A couple of years later, Tony was giving a lecture in Miami Beach. He submitted a proposal to the state of Florida to salvage a virgin 1733 shipwreck in the Florida Keys. It was in the newspapers. He was going to speak to a group in Miami Beach about it," Weller said.

Frank Allen, a friend of Weller's, wanted Weller to attend the lecture with him. Frank was the vice president of Mel Fisher's Treasure Salvors.

"The room had two hundred people in it. Frank and I sat in the front row. Tony Clausen and two other guys were sitting on a little platform. Tony put a chart on the wall. He got up and was exhorting the virtue of the untouched 1733 shipwreck. I don't think he was into the talk two or three minutes when Frank Allen

stood up. He was vice president of Treasure Salvors, Mel Fisher's company and Mel's right hand man," Bob said.

"Frank was very abrupt. He said to Clausen, 'You have no right whatsoever to work that wreck. Bob Weller found it, and if anyone should work it, he should. You never salvaged a wreck before; you don't have the experience and don't have financial backing.'"

Weller smiled, "Tony Clausen walked around the front of the stage and he and Allen, both very big men, got into a heated argument. I said, 'Let's get out of here.' I took Frank by the arm and we left."

Weller was sitting in a soft leather sofa in his office at his home in Lake Worth. The walls were decorated with his framed collection of Spanish navigational dividers, a complete collection of dated one-reale silver cobs, a coffee table covered with a glass top containing a treasure trove from his many exploits. The far wall held his U.S. Navy medals and insignia from his service in World War II and Korea. He was a Lieutenant Commander in the Navy and became the Commanding Officer of Underwater Demolition Team One (UDT 1) in combat.

Weller became angry as he remembered the turmoil the incident caused. "The state did not get the project funded, and the *San Francisco* slept another fifteen years, I guess. Richard MacAllaster [who had a full-time job with Florida's Department of Transportation as head of their bridge system in the Keys and a treasure diver] was probably the first one to put a metal detector on the *San Francisco*, and he picked up 400 coins in a sand pocket away from the ballast pile. Jack Haskins found an emerald ring. I worked it a little bit," Weller said.

His mood changed and a big smile came across his face. Weller is an affable sort who never lets anything get him down for long. His enthusiasm, great energy, and encyclopedic knowledge of Spanish shipwrecks draw many salvors to him for advice.

"I got hit in the head with a cannon ball," Weller smiled broadly, and it was clear a story was building. "There were a lot of six-pound cannon balls on the *San Francisco* site. I used to bring home fifteen, sixteen every time I went out there," he said.

"I came up to *Pandion* with two six-pound cannon balls. I put them up on the dive platform and went back down. The wreck is six feet deep there. Betty and Margaret walked to the stern of *Pandion* to see what it was. When they did, the cannon balls rolled off the stern, and one of them hit me in the head on the way down. It made a thunk," he laughed as he recalled the incident.

"I looked down and saw green in the water. I came up and said, 'Put these two cannon balls in the boat and keep them there.' They said, 'You're bleeding, you're bleeding.' So that's how I got shot with a cannon ball from the *San Francisco*." Weller concluded his story with a laugh.

The merchant nao *San Francisco* displaced 265 tons. It was built in England and purchased by Spanish owners. Letters in the Spanish archives located the *San Francisco* as grounded on Cayo de Vibora, Long Key. Records revealed that the Spanish recovered

19,934 pesos of silver of the 20,000 registered aboard. The contraband in treasure and personal property of passengers and crew was not logged in records in the archives of Spain.

The *Sueco de Arizon* became a fete, celebrated by Weller and his team. It was a treasure diver's dream come true, a fantasy treasure-trove under the sea.

Nuestra Señora del Rosario San Antonio y San Vincente Ferrer, the ship owned by Don Jacinto de Arizon and captained by Don Juan de Arizon, was called simply the ship of Arizon, or the *Sueco de Arizon*. How much easier to note than the whole name of the vessel. Surely as scribes painstakingly drew up manifests and official fleet documents with quill pens and ink, it became their shorthand notation of the time.

The *Sueco de Arizon* is the name used by Bob Weller and teams of divers who sought to recover what Spanish salvors missed after the 1733 hurricane.

It wasn't until 1963 that Mel Fisher moved to Florida. During the next few years he earned fame for discoveries of gold he was making on the 1715 fleet off the area from Vero Beach to Sebastian. Mel obtained salvage leases in the Florida Keys. Weller and Fisher struck a deal. Weller would subcontract the *Sueco de Arizon* site located about a cable length off Crawl Key.

Records of the crown revealed that the *Sueco de Arizon* loaded 24,000 pesos of silver, the usual cargo of leather hides, dyes, and boxes of Chinese porcelain, as well as tobacco, put aboard when the ship made port in Havana after the trip from Veracruz. Salvors have found no record of the *Arizon's* construction. When the hurricane winds subsided the *Arizon* was grounded in nine feet of water without masts or rudder.

It was an easy salvage for the Spanish. The *Arizon's* hull remained intact off what is now called Duck Key and Walker's Key. When Bob Weller and his team first visited the wreck site of the *Sueco*, they measured the ballast pile. It was sixty by twenty feet and about three-and-a-half feet high. Weller described it as a virgin wreck site with iron fittings fused to the untouched ballast stones.

Weller and his team recovered silver pieces of eight by the bucketful. They found 1732 pillar dollars, a date that was a rare numismatic find at the time. It was a time of exhilaration for the team. They celebrated with champagne toasts, piling the silver coins in stacks, counting and recounting them before sealing them in envelopes for an eventual division of shares.

Treasure Beach

Brad Johnson is an enthusiastic treasure diver who has worked on Bob and Margaret Weller's team over several seasons. He bought and refitted *Pandion*, the Weller's legendary treasure hunting ship. Brad studied shipwrecks that the Wellers worked as subcontractors with the Fisher group, who held leases from the state of Florida.

"Let's go to Treasure Beach," Brad suggested to me when I visited him. "Every time I go down there I find something." Brad had

Sextant covered with marine growth.

been very lucky. While searching a spit of beach on the ocean side of U.S. 1, the road from Homestead to Key West, he found coins and a small gold pendant studded with four emeralds in the sand. Brad had a penchant for finding lost treasure, but there was something special about Treasure Beach.

"A man just called me from the Keys," Bob Weller smiled. "He just found a nicely dated cob coin on Treasure Beach." Another clue to what must have occurred offshore in 1733.

The narrow, quarter moon–shaped piece of land between the Gulf and the Atlantic is a catch basin for treasure that washed overboard from the wreck of the *San Felipe*, known as *El Lerri*. The merchant nao belonged to the Marques de Canada. The *El Lerri* displaced 486 tons, a large ship for its time. Like many

Gold and emerald jewelry found by Brad Johnson on Treasure Beach in the Florida Keys.

Divers Hank Haardt (dark sunglasses) and Bill Cassinelli with silver 1732 pillar dollars Bill found while using his metal detector on Treasure Beach. The coins were the first examples of screw press minted coins made in the New World. Previously the Spanish made cob coins cut roughly to weight from a silver bar and stamped with dyes.

galleons that sailed under Spanish ownership, the vessel was made in England.

Archive records indicate that *El Lerri* shipped 34,000 pesos of silver from Veracruz, worked silver along with the dyes, molasses, cocoa, and tobacco from Cuba. The ship sank at a place the Spanish called Cayo de Viboras known also as Matecumbe Nuevo, which is today Lower Matecumbe Key.

Salvors that worked the *El Lerri* ballast pile site, located in about eighteen feet of water, originally measured it at a hundred by forty feet and five feet high off the sand. Divers who seriously worked the ballast pile recovered few coins, although Spanish records indicate that 11,708 pesos of silver were not recovered from El Lerri in the original Spanish salvage effort.

On one trip to Treasure Beach I searched with treasure hunter Hank Haardt. I found nothing, but Hank got a hit with his metal detector. "Take a look?" Diver Hank Haardt held out his hand. He had a small finger-size oblong of silver metal. Hank's hands were black

Bob Weller and veteran treasure diver Bert Kilbride with Weller's 7.4-pound gold disk.

from handling pieces of corroded iron he discovered with his metal detector along Treasure Beach. "Think this was a coin?" Hank asked.

The round object Hank held was so thin and had been worked back and forth in the surf so long that the only resemblance the chip in Hank's hand had to a coin was that it was round.

"I never found a coin here," Hank Haardt lamented. "I took Brad here, I took other guys here. They found coins on the beach right there," Hank pointed to a chunk of concrete near the water line on the beach. It turned out that the chip Hank found was not a cob coin but rather very badly deteriorated modern quarter.

While Hank and I had no luck on Treasure Beach that day, in that very same spot another member of the Weller team of divers a week before found two coins stuck together. When Bill Cassinelli separated the coins, he discovered they were rare 1732 pillar dollars. The insides of the coins where they were stuck together were perfect; the outsides were unrecognizable after centuries in the sand and surf.

"It is likely that passengers' baggage washed overboard during the hurricane and it ended up on the beach here," Brad said, fortunate to have found a small remnant from the shipwreck.

The Almiranta

The king's Almiranta, *El Gallo Indiano*, sporting the name *The Cock of the Indies*, mounted sixty cannons. This ship carried the bulk of the treasure with 5,654,979 pesos of silver coins in bags and boxes. *El Gallo* would bring up the rear of the convoy and protect any ships that

Art McKee's son, Kevin, with the mystery treasure chest. Kevin points to the secret plate, below, which is a key hole.

would become disabled or slowed during the voyage. When the hurricane struck, *El Gallo* was thrown into what is known today as Hawk Channel between Craig Key and Long Key. It sank in fourteen feet of water.

Documents preserved in Spanish archives report that a child, two sailors, and a soldier were killed. Salvage by the Spanish recovered all of the manifested silver coins and much of the other cargo, leaving seventy-nine ingots of copper from the mines of Cuba.

Modern-day salvors recovered ship's utensils and accoutrements from the site of *El Gallo*, but many bypassed the ship as having been salvaged by the Spanish. A ship of that size will offer up evidence of life during the time of Spanish conquest, and if ever a complete archaeological survey and recovery is undertaken, many artifacts will be found underwater. The same is true for other vessels of the 1733 fleet, lost to time.

The loss of the treasure fleet of Don Rodrigo de Torres y Morales, its subsequent salvage by the Spanish, the burning of many of the ships to the waterline and their abandonment to teredo worms, and the tempests of the ocean are the stuff of poetic dreams—a treasure trove under the sea.

Modern-day adventurers and explorers have tempted ocean currents and underwater reaches of the Florida Keys to salvage some of what remains of these fabled treasure-laden galleons.

It is evident that what was scattered by the fury of nature over leagues of ocean can never be fully found or recovered. There will always be those who dream of finding sunken treasure. Chance discoveries along the shore in places like Treasure Beach, finding artifacts and coins from the shipwrecks of 1733, can make those dreams come true. 🐚

Some of the treasures recovered by Brad Johnson from the 1733 fleet.

Wooden ships and iron men, in the days of sail when navigators could only guess their general position and predict weather by superstition.

BIBLIOGRAPHY

Amundson, Katherine. *The Story of the Spanish Galleon Nuestra Senora de Atocha*. Key West, FL: Salvors, Inc., 1987.

Anderson, Nina and William. *Southern Treasures*. Chester, CT: Globe Pequot Press Press, 1987.

Bankson, Ross. *Hidden Treasures of the Sea*. Washington DC: National Geographic Society, 1988.

Bascom, Willard. *The Great Wave: Adventures in Oceanography*. New York: Harper & Row, 1988.

Bass, George F. *Archaeology Beneath The Sea*. New York: Walker & Co., 1975.

———. *Archaeology Under Water*. London: Thames & Hudson, 1966.

———. *A History of Seafaring Based On Underwater Archaeology*. London: Thames & Hudson, 1972.

———. *Ships and Shipwrecks of North America*. London: Thames & Hudson, 1988.

Bischoff, William L. *The Coinage of El Peru*. New York: The American Numismatic Society, 1989.

Blassingame, Wyatt. *Diving for Treasure*. Philadelphia: Macrae-Smith Co., 1971.

Blot, Jean-Yves. *Underwater Archaeology: Exploring the World Beneath the Sea*. Paris: Editions Gallimard, 1995.

Bound, Mensun. *The Archaeology of Ships of War*. Shropshire, UK: Anthony Nelson, Ltd., 1995.

———. *Lost Ships*. New York: Simon & Schuster, 1998.

Breeden, R. L., and D. J. Crump. *Undersea Treasures*. Washington, DC: National Geographic Society, 1974.

Brown, Joseph E. *The Golden Sea: Man's Underwater Adventures*. New York: The Playboy Press, 1974.

Budde-Jones, Kathryn. *Coins of the Lost Galleons*. Self-published, 1993.

Buranelli, Vincent. *Gold: An Illustrated History*. Maplewood, NJ: Hammond, Inc., 1979.

Burgess, Robert F. *Gold, Galleons & Archaeology*. Indianapolis, IN: Bobbs-Merrill Co., 1976.

———. *Man: 12,000 Years Under the Sea*. New York: Dodd Mead & Co., 1980.

———. *Sinkings, Salvages and Shipwrecks*. New York: American Heritage Press, 1970.

Burton, Hal. *The Real Book about Treasure Hunting*. Garden City, NY: Garden City Books, 1953.

Castillo, Bernal Diaz del. *The Discovery and Conquest of Mexico*. New York: Farrar, Straus and Cudahy, 1956.

Chorlton, Windsor. *Buried & Sunken Treasure*. London: Marshall Cavendish, 1974.

Codinach, Guadalupe Jimenez. *The Hispanic World 1492–1898*. Washington, DC: Library of Congress, 1994.

Coffman, F. L. *Atlas of Treasure Maps*. New York: Thomas Nelson & Sons, 1957.

Craig, Alan K. *Gold Coins of the 1715 Spanish Plate Fleet*. Tallahassee, FL: Florida Bureau of Archaeological Research, 1988.

Deagan, Kathleen. *Artifacts of the Spanish Colonies of Florida & Caribbean, 1500–1800.* Washington, DC: Smithsonian Institution Press, 1987.

Dean, Martin et al. *Archaeology Underwater: The NAS Guide to Principles and Practice.* London: Nautical Archaeological Society, 1992.

Delgado, James P. *Encyclopedia of Underwater and Maritime Archaeology.* New Haven, CT: Yale University Press, 1998.

DuBois, Bessie Wilson. *Shipwrecks in the Vicinity of Jupiter Island.* Jupiter, FL: Pamphlet published by the author, 1975.

Dumas, Frederic. *Thirty Centuries Under the Sea.* New York: Crown Publishers, 1976.

Fine, John Christopher. *Lost on the Ocean Floor.* Annapolis, MD: U.S. Naval Institute Press, 2005.

———. *Sunken Ships & Treasures.* New York: Atheneum-Macmillan, 1986.

———. *Sunken Treasure.* New York: Richard C. Owen, Publishers, 2000.

Garrett, Charles. *Treasure Recovery from Sand and Sea.* Dallas, TX: Ram Books, 1988.

Horner, Dave. *The Treasure Galleons.* New York: Dodd Meade & Co., 1971.

Lane, W. H. & Son. *Gold & Silver Treasure.* Plymouth, UK: W. H. Lane & Son, 1979.

Lincoln, Margarette. *Shipwrecks: Learning Through Underwater Archaeology.* Greenwich, UK: National Maritime Museum, 1993.

Lyon, Eugene. *The Search for the Atocha.* New York: Harper & Row, 1979.

———. *Search for the Mother Lode of the Atocha.* Port Salerno, FL: Florida Calssics Library, 1989.

Marken, Mitchell W. *Pottery from Spanish Shipwrecks 1500–1800.* Gainesville, FL: University Press of Florida, 1994.

Marx, Robert F. *The History of Underwater Exploration.* New York: Dover Publications, 1990.

———. *In the Wake of the Galleons.* Flagstaff, AZ: Best Publications, 2001.

———. *Into the Deep: The History of Man's Underwater Exploration.* New York: Van Nostrand Reinhold Co., 1978.

———. *Spanish Treasure In Florida Waters.* Boston: Mariners Press, 1979.

Marx, Robert F., and Jennifer Marx. *Shipwrecks of the Western Hemisphere.* Cleveland: World Publishing Co., 1971.

McKee, Alexander. *History Under The Sea.* London: Hutchinson & Co., 1968.

Peterson, Mendel. *The Funnels of Gold.* Boston: Little Brown & Co., 1975.

———. *History Under The Sea.* Washington, DC: Smithsonian Institution, 1965.

Potter, John S. *The Treasure Diver's Guide.* Garden City, NY: Doubleday & Co., 1960.

Pradeau, Alberto-Francisco. *Numismatic History of Mexico.* New York: Sanford J. Durst, 1978.

Reisberg, Harry E. *The Sea of Treasure.* New York: Frederick Fell, Inc., 1966.

Sedwick, Frank. *The Practical Book of Cobs.* Maitland, FL: self-published, 1987.

Silverberg, Robert. *Sunken History: The Story of Underwater Archaeology.* Philadelphia: Chilton Books, 1963.

Singer, Steven D. *Shipwrecks of Florida.* Sarasota, FL: Pineapple Press, 1992.

Throckmorton, Peter. *The Lost Ships*. Boston: Little, Brown & Co., 1964.

———. *Shipwrecks and Archaeology*. Boston: Little, Brown & Co., 1970.

Wagner, Kip, and L. B. Taylor. *Pieces of Eight*. New York: E.P. Dutton & Co., 1966.

Weller, Robert. *The Dreamweaver*. Charleston, SC: Fletcher Publishing, 1966.

———. *Galleon Alley: The 1733 Spanish Treasure Fleet*. Lake Worth, FL: Crossed Anchors Salvage, Inc. 2001.

———. *Galleon Hunt*. Lake Worth, FL: Crossed Anchors Salvage, Inc., 1992.

———. *Salvaging Spanish Sunken Treasure*. Lake Worth, FL: Crossed Anchors Salvage Inc., 1999.

———.*Sunken Treasure on Florida Reefs*. Lake Worth, FL: Crossed Anchors Salvage, 1987.

INDEX